Introduction to the Command Line

The <u>Fat-Free</u> Guide to Unix and Linux Commands

Second Edition

Introduction to the Command Line
The Fat-Free Guide to Unix and Linux Commands
Second Edition (Rev 2)

ISBN: 1450588301
EAN-13: 9781450588300

www.DontFearTheCommandLine.com

Questions or comments? Email grepnick@gmail.com

Contents at a Glance

Table of Contents

Section 6: Process Control and Scheduling................... 115

"UNIX is basically a simple operating system, but you have to be a genius to understand the simplicity."

— Dennis Ritchie

Creator of the C programming language and co-creator of UNIX

Introduction

The command line can be an intimidating and unforgiving environment. Unlike working in graphical environments, it's not entirely clear what commands one must execute in a terminal to accomplish a given task. Couple this with the fact that the command line does not prevent you from doing things that might cause irreparable damage to your system, and it becomes clear why many people never take the time to learn how to use it.

Despite the hidden dangers and uncertainty faced by new users (known jokingly as "newbies" in the technology industry), you shouldn't fear the command line. Armed with the information in this book you will acquire the skills necessary to become more proficient in the command line environment. You will discover that most Unix, Linux, and BSD systems share the same core architecture, with only a few subtle differences. After learning the basic architecture and commands of Unix, Linux, and BSD systems you will easily be able to transition between the different platforms.

To aid the learning process, I recommend downloading one or more of the free operating systems listed below to practice the commands in this guide.

Operating System	Type	Website
Ubuntu	Linux	www.ubuntu.com
Fedora	Linux	www.fedoraproject.org
CentOS	Linux	www.centos.org
openSUSE	Linux	www.opensuse.org
OpenSolaris	Unix	www.opensolaris.org
FreeBSD	BSD	www.freebsd.org

It's a worthwhile experience to experiment with multiple Unix, Linux, and BSD distributions to get a broader knowledge of the various platforms. This will help expand your knowledge of the various Unix-like operating systems and give you the skills necessary to work in any command line environment.

Linux is the recommended starting point for beginners. It has support for all the latest hardware and provides a user-friendly installation process. The OpenSolaris

Unix platform is also a good starting point, as it is one of the most newbie-friendly Unix-based systems. BSD installation is a bit more challenging and requires advanced technical knowledge or previous experience with Unix and Linux systems.

Tip	*I highly recommend Ubuntu Server Edition. It provides an easy install experience and an excellent command line learning environment. Visit www.ubuntu.com for more information about the Ubuntu Server Linux distribution.*

If you are a Microsoft Windows user, you may already have some command line experience. If you have ever opened a DOS prompt and executed a command such as `ping`, `nslookup`, or `ipconfig` then you know these can be immensely helpful. Unix, Linux, and BSD systems offer similar commands. For example, the `ping` and `nslookup` commands work the same on Unix/Linux as they do in DOS. You should note, however, that the DOS `ipconfig` command's counterpart in the Unix/Linux/BSD world is `ifconfig`. If you're not a DOS veteran, don't worry - we will cover all of these topics throughout this guide.

Are you running Mac OS X? If so, then you are already running a Unix-based operating system. Behind the shiny graphical user interface of Mac OS X is a solid Unix core. To access the command line in Mac OS X simply launch the Terminal application (located in **Applications > Utilities > Terminal**). From there you will have access to all the standard Unix command line utilities discussed in this guide.

Brief History of Unix, Linux, and BSD

Unix was created in 1969 at Bell Laboratories which was, at the time, a research and development division of AT&T. Since that time, Unix has branched into many different commercial and open source implementations, most of which are based on the original AT&T standard. Modern Unix-based systems are typically classified into one of the following groups:

Unix	*Commercial implementations derived from the original AT&T code base*
BSD	*Open source operating system derived from the original Unix code base*
Linux	*Open source Unix compatible clone written from scratch*

In the 1970s, researchers at the University of California, Berkeley began developing BSD (short for **B**erkeley **S**oftware **D**istribution). BSD was originally based on the AT&T Unix codebase, but has been rewritten over time to remove AT&T copyrighted code from the system. This allows BSD to be distributed with minimal restrictions. Since that time, the BSD code-base has split to form a number of popular operating systems including FreeBSD, OpenBSD, and NetBSD. BSD code can also be found in proprietary proprietary operating systems created by Microsoft, Apple, and Sun Microsystems.

Commercial Unix systems began to appear in the early 1980s. These systems combined various amounts of Unix and BSD code along with vendor-specific enhancements to create new platforms such as AIX, HP-UX, and Sun Solaris. Today, commercial Unix systems can be found in data centers at many large companies running mission critical applications.

In 1991, a computer science student at the University of Helsinki in Finland named Linus Torvalds created the Linux operating system. While Linux shares much of the core concepts of Unix, it contains no Unix code. This means it can be freely distributed in the same manner as BSD (although under a different license). The first commercial Linux distributions hit the market in the mid 1990s. Since then hundreds of Linux variants have been developed. The open nature of the Linux operating system has contributed to its success and helped make it one of the most popular server operating systems in use today.

The Unix platform has been around since long before graphical user interfaces were invented. The fact that Unix-based systems are still a commanding force in modern computing is a testament to the industrial design of the platform. With Unix, Linux, and BSD popularity at an all time high, now is the perfect time to explore these platforms and join the movement.

Conventions Used in This Book

`/path/to/file`

File and directory paths are displayed in a fixed width font

`command`

Commands are displayed in a bold fixed width font

`[FILE]`, `[DIRECTORY]`, `[ETC]`

Items enclosed in brackets represent a variable parameter to be specified by the user (such as a file or directory)

```
$ ping 192.168.1.1
```

Examples using the $ shell prompt are executed with a non-privileged user account

```
# ping 192.168.1.1
```

Examples using the # shell prompt are executed at the root user

```
...
```

Additional command output truncated (to save space)

```
$ whe<TAB>
```

Items enclosed in <> indicate an action key such as <TAB>, <ESC>, <SPACE>, etc.

Section 1: Overview of Unix, Linux and BSD Architecture

The Kernel

At the heart of every Unix, Linux, and BSD system is the kernel. The kernel provides a layer between the computer hardware and user applications. When applications need to display output to a screen or write files to the disk, the kernel facilitates these actions. Think of the kernel as the conductor in a symphony; it directs all the actions of the operating system.

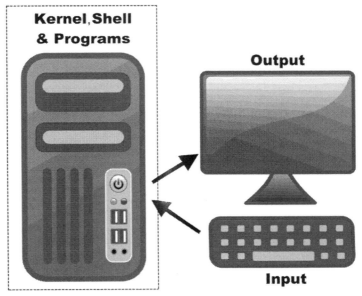

Overview of the Kernel

When you type a command on the keyboard, the computer hardware receives the signals and transfers them to the kernel. The kernel recognizes the key strokes and draws them on the display. Once the typed command is executed, the program will utilize the kernel to request processor, memory, and other resources in order to perform the requested task.

Popular Versions of Unix, Linux, and BSD

There are many different Unix, Linux, and BSD distributions. The tables below list the most popular systems in use today.

BSD Systems

OS	Description
Darwin	BSD-based core of the Mac OS X operating system
FreeBSD	User friendly BSD-based operating system
OpenBSD	Security focused BSD-based operating system
NetBSD	Highly portable BSD-based operating system

Linux Systems

OS	Description
Red Hat Enterprise Linux	Popular commercial Linux distribution created by Red Hat, Inc.
Fedora	Free community-based distribution that serves as a test bed for new technologies that feed into Red Hat Enterprise Linux
CentOS	Free binary-compatible clone of Red Hat Enterprise Linux
Debian	Popular non-commercial Linux distribution
Ubuntu	User-friendly Linux distribution based on Debian
SuSE Enterprise Linux	Commercial Linux distribution created by Novell, Inc.
openSUSE	Free community-based distribution based on SUSE Enterprise Linux

Unix Systems

OS	Description
AIX	IBM's proprietary Unix platform
HP-UX	Hewlett Packard's proprietary Unix platform
Solaris	Sun Microsystems' proprietary Unix platform
OpenSolaris	Open source version of the Solaris operating system

> **Note** *Other notable Unix platforms include SGI IRIX, Compaq Tru64, and SCO UnixWare/OpenServer; however, these systems are no longer widely used or supported.*

Unix, Linux, and BSD Directory Structure

Most Unix, Linux, and BSD systems share a similar directory structure. The table below lists the main directories commonly used across all platforms.

Directory	Purpose
`/`	Root (top level) directory
`/boot`	Linux kernel and boot loader files

`/stand`
`/unix`
`/vmunix`
`/kernel`
	Unix kernel directories

`/bin`
`/usr`
`/usr/bin`
	Core binary programs for normal users

`/sbin` `/usr/sbin`	Administrative programs primarily used by the root user
`/opt`	Optional add-on/third-party software
`/etc`	System configuration files
`/home`	User home directories
`/root`	Home directory of the root user
`/lib`	Shared libraries used by various programs
`/media` `/mnt`	Mounted local and remote file systems
`/var`	Variable data (such as system logs) that changes often
`/tmp`	Temporary files used by various programs
`/dev`	Device files
`/sys`	Virtual device driver files used by the kernel
`/proc`	Virtual parameter and informational files used by the kernel
`/lost+found`	Files that have been recovered (after a system failure)

Unix, Linux, and BSD directory structure

These directories are organized in a manner which separates various components of the operating system in an easy to manage file structure. The `/home` directory is where users spend most of their time. Files outside of this directory are usually secured so that only the root user can edit or delete them. This protects vital programs and configuration files and prevents users from accidently damaging the core operating system. It also helps secure the system by preventing malicious programs from being able to compromise critical files and settings.

Important Files

In addition to sharing a similar directory structure, most systems will also have the important files listed in following table.

File	Purpose
/etc/passwd	User account settings
/etc/shadow	Encrypted passwords for user accounts
/etc/group	Group settings
/etc/fstab	Local file system settings
/etc/mtab	Mounted file systems
/etc/inittab	System startup settings
/etc/exports	NFS share settings
/etc/hosts	Static name resolution file
/etc/hostname	System host name setting
/etc/hosts.allow	Network hosts allowed to connect to the system
/etc/resolv.conf	DNS settings
/etc/hosts.deny	Network hosts not allowed to connect to the system
/etc/issue	Message displayed at shell login
/etc/issue.net	Remote login message
/etc/motd	Message displayed after logging in
/etc/profile	Shell environment settings
/etc/shells	Valid shells permitted to login
/etc/sudoers	Users allowed to use the su command (discussed on page 99)
/var/log/messages	Kernel messages log file
/var/log/wtmp	Current user login log file
/var/log/lastlog	User login history log file
/var/log/kern.log	Kernel log file
/var/log/syslog	Syslog messages log file

Important files

This is just a brief list of the most commonly used files shared across most platforms. As a general rule, configuration files are located in the /etc directory and system logs are stored in /var/log. As you become more familiar with Unix, Linux, and BSD systems you will begin working with these files to manage system configuration and troubleshoot problems.

Common Unix, Linux, and BSD File Systems

Unix, Linux, and BSD share support for several types of file systems. The table below provides a matrix of the most common file systems and their supported platforms.

	AIX	HP-UX	Solaris	BSD	Linux
EXT2-4	Partial	No	Partial	Partial	Yes
JFS (IBM)	Yes	No	No	No	Yes
HFS+	No	No	No	No	Partial
UFS	No	Yes	Yes	Yes	Partial
VxFS	Yes	Yes	Yes	No	Yes
ZFS	No	No	Yes	Yes	Yes

File system support matrix

EXT versions 2 through 4 are file systems used by the Linux operating system. Currently, ext3 is the most widely used file system on Linux distributions. The recently released ext4 file system has many new features and performance benefits over ext3. It will become the default file system for most Linux systems within the next few years. Versions before ext3 are considered obsolete and are rarely used.

JFS is IBM's journaling file system primarily used on the AIX operating system.

HFS+ is Apple's file system used on their Unix-based Mac OS X operating system. HFS+ isn't widely supported by other operating systems but it can be mounted as read-only on Linux systems.

UFS is a Unix file system used primarily by BSD distributions.

VxFS is a file system developed by Veritas Software Corporation (now known as Symantec) and used on HP-UX systems. It is also supported on several other Unix and Linux systems although it is rarely used outside of HP-UX.

ZFS is a new and highly robust file system developed by Sun Microsystems. It is primarily used on the Solaris operating system but also has limited support for some Linux and BSD systems.

Devices

Every Unix, Linux, and BSD system has a directory that is known as `/dev`. This directory contains device files (sometime referred to as special files) that represent hardware installed on the system such as `/dev/mouse` and `/dev/cdrom`.

```
# ls -l /dev/
crw-rw----+ 1 root audio  14,  12 2010-04-22 16:30 adsp
crw-------  1 root video  10, 175 2010-04-22 11:30 agpgart
crw-rw----+ 1 root audio  14,   4 2010-04-22 16:30 audio
crw-rw----  1 root root   10,  59 2010-04-22 11:30 binder
drwxr-xr-x  2 root root      700 2010-04-22 16:30 block
drwxr-xr-x  3 root root       60 2010-04-22 11:30 bus
lrwxrwxrwx  1 root root        3 2010-04-22 16:30 cdrom -> sr0
lrwxrwxrwx  1 root root        3 2010-04-22 16:30 cdrw -> sr0
drwxr-xr-x  2 root root     3220 2010-04-22 16:30 char
crw-------  1 root root    5,   1 2010-04-23 07:36 console
lrwxrwxrwx  1 root root       11 2010-04-22 16:30 core -> /proc/kcore
crw-rw----  1 root root   10,  58 2010-04-22 11:30 cpu_dma_latency
drwxr-xr-x  6 root root      120 2010-04-22 11:30 disk
drwxr-xr-x  2 root root       80 2010-04-22 11:30 dri
crw-rw----+ 1 root audio  14,   3 2010-04-22 16:30 dsp
lrwxrwxrwx  1 root root        3 2010-04-22 16:30 dvd -> sr0
...
```

Example listing of devices in the /dev directory

Within the `/dev` directory there can be several hundred files. Most of these files are of little use in everyday activities. As the system administrator of a Unix or Linux system you will primarily be working with the device files that represent your disk drive(s). Knowing the path to your hard drive is important when working with commands related to file systems. More on this topic is covered in Section 10 of this guide.

> **Note** *Device naming conventions used in* `/dev` *vary across each distribution.*

Within `/dev`, there are also a few helpful pseudo-devices. Pseudo-devices do not represent actual hardware and exist only to perform a specific task. The table below describes the most commonly used pseudo-devices.

File	Purpose
`/dev/zero`	File that produces a continuous stream of 0-byte characters
`/dev/random`	Random number generator
`/dev/null`	Special file that discards any data written to it

The Shell

The command line interpreter, also known as the shell, is a program that accepts input from a user (typically a command of some sort) and performs the requested task. Once that task has completed, the program will terminate and return the user to the shell.

The shell's prompt identifies the type of shell being used. There are two basic types of shell prompts:

$ Normal user shell   (may also be % or > on some systems)
#   Root user shell

Below is the output of the `whoami` command (discussed on page 102) which highlights the difference between normal user and root shell prompts on the command line.

```
$ whoami
nick
```
Normal user shell

```
# whoami
root
```
Root user shell

Normal users typically have a limited amount of access to the system while the root user has unrestricted access. Section 5 covers this topic in more detail.

Warning	*The root user can do <u>anything</u> on Unix, Linux, and BSD systems. It is important to know when you are working as root to prevent accidental damage to your system.*

Many systems add customized information to the shell prompt. This information can be a handy indicator of things like the current user's login name, system host name, and the current directory as shown in the next example.

```
nick@mylaptop:/var/log $
```
Example of a customized shell prompt

The table below describes the information displayed in the customized shell prompt displayed in the previous example.

nick	**@**	**mylaptop**	**:**	**/var/log**	**$**
User Name	Spacer	Computer Name	Spacer	Current Directory	Shell Prompt

Types of Shells

There are several different types of shells for Unix, Linux, and BSD systems. Each shell has its own set of features and usage syntax. The next table describes the most popular shells that are currently available.

Shell	Prompt	Name	Notes
sh	$	Borne Shell	Default on some Unix systems
bash	$	Borne Again Shell	Enhanced replacement for the Borne shell
			Default on most Linux and Mac OS X systems
csh	%	C Shell	Default on many BSD systems
tcsh	>	T C Shell	Enhanced replacement for the C shell
ksh	$	Korn shell	Default on AIX systems

Types of shells

The **bash** shell is the most popular shell in use today. It is the default shell on all Linux systems and is also available for most Unix and BSD systems. Other shells like **csh**, **tcsh**, and **ksh** are typically used by default on non-Linux systems.

Accessing the Shell

When you first boot your system you are presented with a login prompt similar to the example pictured below.

```
Ubuntu Linux 9.04

Login: nick
Password: ******

$
```

After you enter your username and password the system will authenticate your login credentials via the /etc/passwd file. If the login information is correct, the system will start your shell (which is also specified in /etc/passwd). The $ shell prompt indicates you are logged in and "ready to go."

Welcome to the world of the command line... Let's get started!

Section 2:
Command Line Basics

Overview

This section covers the most essential commands every user should know. These basic commands cover topics like getting help, navigating directories, and listing files. Before you begin, there are three important rules you need to know about the command line:

1. Unix, Linux, and BSD systems are case (and space) sensitive. This means that a file named `MyFile` is not same as `myfile` as it would be on a DOS or Windows system.
2. There is no "recycle bin" or "trash can" when working in the command line environment. When files are deleted on the command line, they instantly disappear forever.
3. You should always practice new commands on a testing system that is not used in a production environment. This minimizes the chances of an accident that can take down an important system.

Knowing this, we can now begin working with basic Unix, Linux and BSD commands.

Note	*Examples listed in this book were created on various Unix, Linux, and BSD systems. Many of the commands, options, and features are the same on other platforms; however, there may be slight differences. You should always consult the manual for your specific platform to ensure compatibility with the examples provided. See page 27 for more information on how to access the online manual.*

Commands covered in this section:

Command	Purpose
man	Online manual for command line programs.
whatis	Display a description of the specified command.
ls	List the contents of a directory.
pwd	Display the current/working directory.
cd	Change (navigate) directories.
tree	Display the contents of a directory in a tree hierarchy format.
find	Search for files and directories.
locate	Search the locate database for files and directories.
whereis	Display the location of binary files, manual pages, and source code for the specified command.
file	Display the file type of the specified file.
stat	Display extended information about a file system, file, or directory.
date	Display or set the system clock.
cal	Display a calendar on the command line.
history	Display commands that have recently been executed.
clear	Clear the contents of the current screen.
logout	Logout of the system.
exit	Exit the current shell.

Glossary of terms used in this section:

Argument	One or more variable input items used by a command line program.
Binary	A compiled program or data file.
Flag	Synonym for *Option*.
Man Page	Online manual for shell commands.
Option	A modifier that alters the default operation of a command.
Parameter	Synonym for *Argument*.
Recursively	Includes all subdirectories when executing a command.
Shell Script	A grouping of commands in a plain text executable file.
Source Code	Uncompiled code for a program.
Switch	Synonym for *Option*.
Working Directory	Your current location within the directory tree.

man

Purpose: Online manual for command line programs.

Usage syntax: `man [OPTIONS] [COMMAND/FILE]`

```
$ man ls
LS(1)                          User Commands                          LS(1)

NAME
       ls - list directory contents

SYNOPSIS
       ls [OPTION]... [FILE]...

DESCRIPTION
       List  information  about  the FILEs (the current directory by
       default). Sort entries alphabetically if none of -cftuvSUX nor
       --sort.

       -a, --all
              do not ignore entries starting with .
...
```

Viewing the manual page for the ls command

The `man` command displays the manual (often referred to as the *man page*) for the specified command. Each manual page provides detailed information about a command's options and usage. In the above example, executing `man ls` displays the manual for the `ls` command.

The table below describes the keys that can be used to navigate the manual program.

Key	Function	Key	Function
Up Arrow	Navigate one line up	**Down Arrow**	Navigate one line down
Page Up	Navigate one page up	**Page Down**	Navigate one page down
Q	Quit the `man` program	**/[STRING]**	Search for a string of text

The `man` command is your most valuable resource for help on the command line. Always look to the manual pages for any command if you are unsure of its proper usage syntax.

Common usage examples:

`man [COMMAND]`	Display the manual for the specified command
`man -k [KEYWORD]`	Search manual pages for the specified keyword

whatis

Purpose: Display a description of the specified command.

Usage syntax: whatis [OPTIONS] [COMMAND]

```
$ whatis ls
ls (1)                  - list directory contents
```
Viewing the manual description of the ls command

whatis displays a brief description of the specified command. The above example displays the description of the `ls` command using **whatis**. This can be used as a helpful reminder of a command's purpose without having to refer to the **man** command.

Multiple commands can be used with one **whatis** query to display the description of each individual command. For example, typing **whatis ls who rm** would display the description of all three commands at once as demonstrated in the next example.

```
$ whatis ls who rm
ls (1)                  - list directory contents
who (1)                 - show who is logged on
rm (1)                  - remove files or directories
```
Viewing the manual description of multiple commands

> **Note**   *Some Unix systems may use the* **apropos** *command in place of* **whatis**.

Common usage examples:

whatis [COMMAND]	Display the description of the specified command
whatis -w [WILDCARD]	Search for commands using a wildcard

ls

Purpose: List the contents of a directory.

Usage syntax: `ls [OPTIONS] [DIRECTORY/FILE]`

```
$ ls
Notes.txt   ShoppingList.txt   ToDoList.txt
```
Typical output of the ls command

Executing the `ls` command displays a simple list of files in the current directory, as shown in the above example. To see more information about the files in a directory you can use command line options to activate additional features, as demonstrated in the next example.

```
$ ls -l
-rw-r--r-- 1 nick sales 35068 2009-05-19 08:41 Notes.txt
-rw-r--r-- 1 nick sales    23 2009-05-19 08:43 ShoppingList.txt
-rw-r--r-- 1 nick sales    37 2009-05-19 08:43 ToDoList.txt
```
Using the -l option with the ls command

In this example, the `-l` option is used to produce a detailed list of files including the permissions, owner, group, and modification date/time. The table below describes the output of the `ls -l` command.

Permissions	Number of Links	Owner & Group	Size	Modification Date	File or Directory
`-rw-r--r--`	1	`nick sales`	35068	`2009-05-19 08:41`	`Notes.txt`

Description of fields displayed with the ls -l command

Most command line programs have numerous options available. The `ls` command is no exception. By combining these options you can activate multiple features at the same time. For example, combining the `-a` option with `-l` produces a detailed file list that includes hidden files (files begin with a dot).

```
$ ls -l -a
drwxr-xr-x  2 nick sales  4096 2009-05-19 21:14 .
drwxr-xr-x 92 nick sales  4096 2009-05-19 20:46 ..
-rw-r--r--  1 nick sales   168 2009-05-19 21:14 .MyHiddenFile
-rw-r--r--  1 nick sales 35068 2009-05-19 08:41 Notes.txt
-rw-r--r--  1 nick sales    23 2009-05-19 08:43 ShoppingList.txt
-rw-r--r--  1 nick sales    37 2009-05-19 08:43 ToDoList.txt
```
Using multiple options with the ls command

(Continued...)

Tip	*Most command line options can be combined using shorthand notation. For example,* `ls -l -a` *can be shortened to* `ls -la`.

Note	*Command line options are not universal. Each command has its own set of options that are specific to that program. Additionally, each implementation of the same command on different platforms may use different options. Refer to the man pages for a complete list of command line options supported on your system.*

Common usage examples:

Command	Description
`ls`	Display a basic list of files in the current directory
`ls [DIRECTORY]`	Display a basic list of files in the specified directory
`ls -l`	List files with details
`ls -la`	List hidden files
`ls -lh`	List file sizes in "human readable format" (KB, MB, etc.)
`ls -R`	Recursively list all subdirectories
`ls -d [DIRECTORY]`	List only the specified directory (not its contents)

pwd

Purpose: Display the current/working directory.

Usage syntax: pwd

```
$ pwd
/home/nick
```

Using the pwd command the display the current directory

The **pwd** command (short for **P**rint **W**orking **D**irectory) displays your current location within the file system. In the above example, executing **pwd** displays /home/nick as the current working directory.

Note	Unix, Linux, and BSD systems use a forward slash (i.e. /home/nick) to separate directory names in contrast to MS-DOS and Windows systems which use a back slash (i.e. C:\Windows\system32).

Common usage examples:

pwd | Display the current working directory.

cd

Purpose: Change (navigate) directories.

Usage syntax: `cd [DIRECTORY]`

```
$ cd /etc
$ pwd
/etc
```

Using the cd command to navigate to the /etc directory

The `cd` command (short for **C**hange **D**irectories) changes your location within the file system to the specified path. In the above example, executing `cd /etc` makes `/etc` the new working directory.

The `cd` command interprets directory paths relative to your current location unless you manually specify a full path (such as `cd /etc` as used in the first example.) The next example demonstrates using `cd` to change directories relative to the current location.

```
$ pwd
/home/nick
$ cd documents
$ pwd
/home/nick/documents
```

Using the cd command to navigate to a directory relative to the current location

In this example, the starting directory is `/home/nick`. Typing `cd documents` makes `/home/nick/documents` the new working directory. If you were starting in a different location you would have to type the full path (i.e. `cd /home/nick/documents`) to achieve the same results. Since the previous location was `/home/nick`, typing the full path is not necessary.

Tip	*Executing the* `cd` *command with no options returns you to your home directory regardless of your current location.*

Common usage examples:

`cd [DIRECTORY]`	Navigate to the specified directory
`cd`	Navigate to the user's home directory
`cd -`	Go back to the previous working directory
`cd ..`	Navigate up one level in the directory tree

tree

Purpose: Display the contents of a directory in a tree hierarchy format.

Usage syntax: `tree [OPTIONS] [DIRECTORY]`

```
$ cd /
$ tree -d -L 2
.
|-- bin
|-- boot
|     `-- grub
|-- cdrom -> media/cdrom
|-- dev
|     |-- block
|     |-- bus
|     |-- char
|     |-- disk
|     |-- fd -> /proc/self/fd
|     |-- input
...
|-- etc
|     |-- ConsoleKit
|     |-- NetworkManager
|     |-- PolicyKit
|     |-- X11
|     |-- acpi
|     |-- alsa
|     |-- alternatives
...
```

Tree listing of directory structures

The **tree** command displays a directory listing in tree form. This is useful for visualizing the layout of a directory structure. In the above example, executing **tree -d -L 2** displays 2 directory levels (relative to the current location) in tree form.

Common usage examples:

`tree`	Display the contents of the current directory in tree form
`tree [DIR]`	Display the contents of the specified directory in tree form
`tree -a`	Include hidden files in the tree listing
`tree -d`	List directories only
`tree -L [NUM]`	List the specified number of levels deep

find

Purpose: Search for files and directories.

Usage syntax: find [PATH] [OPTIONS] [CRITERIA]

```
# find / -name hosts
/etc/avahi/hosts
/etc/hosts
/usr/share/hosts
```

Using the find command to locate files with the word "hosts" in their name

The `find` command performs a raw search on a file system to locate the specified items. You can search for files using a number of characteristics - the most common being file name, owner, size, or modification time. The above example displays the results of a search for files that contain the word "hosts" in their file name.

The next example displays the results of a search for files owned by the specified user located within the /var directory.

```
# find /var -user nick
/var/mail/nick
```

Locating files owned by a specific user within the /var directory

Note	Since the `find` command performs a raw search on the file system, results can sometimes be slow. It's a good idea to narrow your search to a specific location instead of the entire file system. This will produce faster results and not bog down the system while searching.

Common usage examples:

find [PATH] -name [NAME]	Find files with the specified name
find [PATH] -user [USERNAME]	Find files owned by the specified user
find [PATH] -size [FILESIZE]	Find files larger than the specified size
find [PATH] -mtime 0	Find files modified in the last 24 hours

locate

Purpose: Search the locate database for files and directories.

Usage syntax: `locate [OPTIONS] [DIRECTORY/FILE]`

```
$ locate hosts
/etc/avahi/hosts
/etc/hosts
/usr/share/hosts
```

Searching the locate database for files that contain the word "hosts" in their name

The `locate` command displays the location of files that match the specified name. While similar to the `find` command, `locate` is significantly faster because it searches a database of indexed filenames rather than performing a raw search of the entire file system. A disadvantage of the `locate` command is the fact that it lacks the ability to search for advanced characteristics such as file owner, size, and modification time.

Most Linux and BSD systems have implemented `locate` in order to provide a quick method to locate files by name without affecting the performance of the system.

Note	The `locate` database is updated daily via an automatically scheduled cron job (discussed on page 130) that indexes all local file systems. By default, this usually happens once a day. This means that results are not updated in real-time and newly created or deleted files may not reflect in the results until the next scheduled update.

Common usage examples:

`locate [FILE]`	Locate the specified file
`locate -i [FILE]`	Ignore case when searching

whereis

Purpose: Display the location of binary files, manual pages, and source code for the specified command.

Usage syntax: whereis [OPTIONS] [COMMAND/FILE]

```
$ whereis ls
ls: /bin/ls /usr/share/man/man1/ls.1.gz
```

Displaying the file locations of the ls program using whereis

whereis displays the file locations for the specified command. In the above example, whereis displays the binary file and manual page location for the ls command.

Note	*If the source code is available,* whereis *will also display the location of the source files for the specified command. Source code is not installed by default on most systems.*

Tip	*The* which *command is similar to* whereis *except it only displays results for binary commands. This is useful when you only care to see the path to the binary file for the specified command. For example, typing* which ls *would display the location of binary the file for the* ls *command. See* man which *for more information.*

Common usage examples:

whereis [COMMAND]	Display the location of the specified command
whereis -b [COMMAND]	Display binary programs only
whereis -m [COMMAND]	Display manual pages only
whereis -s [COMMAND]	Display source code only (if available)

file

Purpose: Display the file type of the specified file.

Usage syntax: `file [OPTIONS] [FILE]`

```
$ file /bin/bash
/bin/bash: ELF 64-bit LSB executable, x86-64, version 1 (SYSV),
dynamically linked (uses shared libs), for GNU/Linux 2.6.15, stripped
$ file /etc/hosts
/etc/hosts: ASCII English text
$ file /home/nick/backup.tgz
backup.tgz: gzip compressed data, from Unix, last modified: Tue May 19
22:29:29 2009
$ file /dev/cdrom
/dev/cdrom: symbolic link to 'sr0'
$ file /dev/sr0
/dev/sr0: block special
```

Using the file command to identify several different types of files

The `file` command displays information about the contents of the specified file. Microsoft Windows systems often use a file extension (such as `.txt`, `.exe`, `.zip`, etc.) to identify the type of data found in a file. Unix, Linux, and BSD files rarely include an extension which can make identifying their file type a challenge. The `file` command is provided to resolve this problem.

The above example displays results for several file types commonly found on Unix, Linux, and BSD systems. The table below displays more information about these file types.

Type	Description
Ascii Text Files	Plain text files
Binary Files	Executable programs such as those located in the `/bin` and `/usr/bin` directories
Compressed Files	Files compressed through the **compress** or **gzip** programs
Device Files	Special virtual files that represent devices
Links	Links (AKA shortcuts) that point to other files or directories

Basic file types found on Unix, Linux, and BSD systems

Common usage examples:

`file [FILE]` | Display the file type for the specified files

stat

Purpose: Display extended information about a file system, file, or directory.

Usage syntax: stat [OPTIONS] [FILE/DIRECTORY]

```
$ stat /etc/hosts
  File: '/etc/hosts'
  Size: 266           Blocks: 8          IO Block: 4096   regular file
Device: 805h/2053d    Inode: 788         Links: 1
Access: (0644/-rw-r--r--)  Uid: (    0/    root)   Gid: (    0/    root)
Access: 2009-05-25 20:47:14.916626707 -0500
Modify: 2009-05-25 20:46:57.512623325 -0500
Change: 2009-05-25 20:46:57.512623325 -0500
```

Displaying information for the /etc/hosts file using the stat command

The **stat** command displays extended information about files. It includes helpful information not available when using the **ls** command such as the file's last access time and technical information about the file's location within the file system. The example above displays the **stat** output for the /etc/hosts file. The next example displays the **stat** output for the /etc directory itself.

```
$ stat /etc
  File: '/etc'
  Size: 4096          Blocks: 8          IO Block: 4096   directory
Device: 801h/2049d    Inode: 316993      Links: 75
Access: (0755/drwxr-xr-x)  Uid: (    0/    root)   Gid: (    0/    root)
Access: 2010-04-01 12:17:44.000000000 -0500
Modify: 2010-03-28 12:47:21.000000000 -0500
Change: 2010-03-28 12:47:21.000000000 -0500
```

Displaying stat output for a directory

The **-f** option can be used with **stat** to display information for an entire file system as shown in the next example.

```
$ stat -f /
  File: "/"
    ID: e708bc097a45b919 Namelen: 255      Type: ext2/ext3
Block size: 4096      Fundamental block size: 4096
Blocks: Total: 9965379      Free: 9723316      Available: 9221085
Inodes: Total: 2514944      Free: 2476388
```

Using the -f option with stat to display information about a file system

Common usage examples:

stat [FILE/DIR]	Display information for the specified file/directory
stat -f [FILESYSTEM]	Display information for the specified file system

date

Purpose: Display or set the system clock.

Usage syntax: `date [OPTIONS] [TIME/DATE]`

```
$ date
Wed Jun 10 20:33:27 CDT 2009
```

Output of the date command

The `date` command displays the current time and date for the local system, as shown in the above example.

Note	Unix, Linux, and BSD systems track time in 24-hour format.

The `-s` option can be used to set the time/date on the system as demonstrated in the next example.

```
# date -s "07/10/2009 11:30"
Fri Jul 10 11:30:00 CDT 2009
```

Setting the time and date

When setting both the time and date you must use `"MM/DD/YYYY HH:MM"` format. To set the time only you can simply use `date -s HH:MM`.

Note	You must login as root or use the `sudo` command (discussed on page 99) to set the system clock.

Common usage examples:

`date`	Display the time and date
`date -s [HH:MM]`	Set the time
`date -s ["MM/DD/YYYY HH:MM"]`	Set the time and date

cal

Purpose: Display a calendar on the command line.

Usage syntax: `cal [OPTIONS] [MONTH] [YEAR]`

```
$ cal
      May 2009
Su Mo Tu We Th Fr Sa
                1  2
 3  4  5  6  7  8  9
10 11 12 13 14 15 16
17 18 19 20 21 22 23
24 25 26 27 28 29 30
31
```
Displaying a calendar for the current month

The `cal` command displays a simple calendar on the command line. Executing `cal` with no arguments will display a calendar for the current month, as shown in the above example. Adding a month and year as arguments will display a calendar for the specified month and year, as shown in the next example.

```
$ cal 8 2009
     August 2009
Su Mo Tu We Th Fr Sa
                   1
 2  3  4  5  6  7  8
 9 10 11 12 13 14 15
16 17 18 19 20 21 22
23 24 25 26 27 28 29
30 31
```
Displaying a calendar for the specified month

Common usage examples:

`cal`	Display a calendar for the current month
`cal -m`	Display Monday as the first day of the week
`cal [MONTH] [YEAR]`	Display a calendar for the specified month and year
`cal [YEAR]`	Display a calendar for the specified year
`cal -y`	Display a calendar for the current year

`history`

Purpose: Display commands that have recently been executed.

Usage syntax: `history [OPTIONS]`

```
$ history 10
  686  man uptime
  687  cat /etc/hosts
  688  ls -l
  689  uptime
  690  dmesg
  691  iostat
  692  vmstat
  693  ping google.com
  694  tracepath google.com
  695  history 10
```

Display 10 lines of command history

The `history` command displays a user's command line history. Executing the `history` command with no arguments will display the entire command line history for the current user. For a shorter list, a number can be specified as an argument. Typing `history 10`, for example, will display the last 10 commands executed by the current user as shown in the above example.

Tip	*You can execute a previous command using* `![NUM]` *where* NUM *is the line number in history you want to recall. For example, executing* `!687` *will rerun the command listed on line 687 in the above example.*

In Linux, each user has a file called `.bash_history` in their home directory that contains their command line history. Unix systems typically store history in a file called `.sh_history` or `.history`.

Note	*The history file may contain sensitive information about commands you have recently executed. Most systems will automatically overwrite command line history after a certain period. To manually erase the history file in your home directory type* `>$HOME/.*history` *on the command line.*

Common usage examples:

`history`	Display the entire command line history
`history [NUM]`	Display the specified number of history items
`history|grep [PATTERN]`	Search history for the specified pattern

clear

Purpose: Clear the contents of the current screen.

Usage syntax: `clear`

```
$ ls -la
drwxr-xr-x  2 nick nick  4096 2009-05-19 21:14 .
drwxr-xr-x 92 nick nick  4096 2009-05-19 20:46 ..
-rw-r--r--  1 nick nick 35068 2009-05-19 08:41 Notes.txt
-rw-r--r--  1 nick nick   168 2009-05-19 21:14 .MyHiddenFile
-rw-r--r--  1 nick nick    23 2009-05-19 08:43 ShoppingList.txt
-rw-r--r--  1 nick nick    37 2009-05-19 08:43 ToDoList.txt
$ clear
```

Screen contents before the clear command is executed

```
$
```

Screen contents after the clear command has been executed

The `clear` command clears the contents of the terminal screen. This is useful for uncluttering the display after you have executed several commands and are preparing to move to the next task. The example above demonstrates the before and after effects of the `clear` command. While clearing the screen after each command isn't necessary, it does make it easier to read the information on the display.

> **Tip**
> **CTRL + L** is a keyboard shortcut to clear the screen in the Bash shell. See Appendix A for more information about Bash shortcut keys.

Common usage examples:

`clear` | Clear the contents of the screen

logout

Purpose: Log out of the system.

Usage syntax: logout

```
$ logout

Ubuntu 9.04

login:
```

Results of the logout command

The logout command logs your account out of the system. This will end your terminal session and return to the login screen.

Some systems may have a file called .logout or .bash_logout in each user's home directory. This file contains commands to be run during the logout process. It is used to perform cleanup operations and clear the screen before ending the user's session.

| Tip | *The logout command is the recommended way to exit the shell. For security purposes, users with administrative access should always logout of any open terminal sessions when away from their desk.* |

Common usage examples:

logout | Log out of the system

exit

Purpose: Exit the current shell.

Usage syntax: exit [CODE]

```
$ exit

login:
```
Example output of the exit command

The `exit` command is similar to the `logout` command with the exception that it does not run the logout script located in the user's home directory. The above example shows the results of exiting the shell and returning to the login prompt.

Shell scripts typically use the `exit` command to properly terminate while users use the `logout` command to properly log out of a system. The exception to this rule is when a terminal application is opened from within a graphical environment on the local system. The `logout` command cannot be used in this situation because terminal session is started as sub shell under the graphical environment. Most systems will display an error in this case as shown in the next example.

```
$ logout
bash: logout: not login shell: use "exit"
```
Logout error message

Tip	**CTRL + D** *is a keyboard shortcut for exiting the shell. See Appendix A for more information on shortcut keys.*

Common usage examples:

exit	Exit the current shell
exit [CODE]	Exit the shell and report an exit code (useful in shell scripting)

Section 3:
Advanced Shell Features
and Commands

Overview

This chapter discusses advanced commands for Unix, Linux, and BSD systems. Advanced commands can be used to perform tasks such as copying, moving, renaming, and deleting files. It will also cover advanced shell features like auto completion, wildcards, pipes, and redirection.

Commands covered in this section:

Command	Purpose
mv	Move or rename files and directories.
cp	Copy files and directories.
rm	Remove files.
mkdir rmdir	Create/remove directories.
touch	Update time stamps on a file.
lsof	List open files.
fuser	Display information about open files.
cksum	Display the checksum of a file.
md5sum	Display the MD5 hash of a file.
ln	Create links (shortcuts) to files or directories.
alias	Create command line aliases.
gzip gunzip	Compress/uncompress files.
split	Split large files into multiple pieces.
shred	Securely erase files.
watch	Periodically execute the specified command.
env	Display environment variables.

Glossary of terms used in this section:

Alias	A shortcut for a command.
Append	Add data to the end of a file instead of overwriting its contents.
Checksum	A data integrity verification algorithm.
Compression	A process used to reduce the size of files.
Interactive	Display confirmation prompts before executing a task.
Link	A shortcut to a file or directory.
MD5 Sum	An enhanced data integrity verification algorithm.
Parent Directory	Higher level directory that contains the current directory.
Pipe	A command line facility that connects the output of one command to the input of another.
Redirection	Command line facilities used to redirect the input or output of a command.
Variable	Adjustable program/environment settings stored in memory.
Verbose	Extended output from a command.
Wildcards	Symbols used to match text patterns.

Auto-Completion

Most shells support command line completion. Command line completion is used to have the shell automatically complete commands or file paths. Command line completion is activated using the **Tab** key on most systems and shown in the following example.

```
$ whe<TAB>
$ whereis
```

Using command line completion

In the above example typing **whe** and pressing the **Tab** key automatically completes the command **whereis** without having to type the entire command.

Auto-completion also works on file paths. Typing `ls -l /etc/en` and pressing the **Tab** key would auto-complete to the file `/etc/environment` as shown in the next example.

```
$ ls -l /etc/en<TAB>
$ ls -l /etc/environment
```

Command line completion of file names

When more than one match is found, the shell will display all matching results. In the next example, typing `ls -l /etc/host` and pressing **Tab** displays all matching files in the `/etc` directory.

```
$ ls -l /etc/host<TAB>
host.conf     hostname      hosts        hosts.allow  hosts.deny
```

Displaying multiple matches using file name completion

> **Tip** *In addition to command line completion, some shells offer the ability to recall previously executed commands by using the **Up Arrow** key on the keyboard.*

Wildcards

Wildcards are used to pattern match one against one or more text elements. They are helpful on the command line for performing bulk tasks such as listing or removing groups of files. The table below lists the different types of wildcards that can be used on the command line.

Wildcard	Function
*	Matches 0 or more characters
?	Matches 1 character
[abc]	Matches one of the characters listed
[a-c]	Matches one character in the range
[!abc]	Matches any character not listed
[!a-c]	Matches any character not listed in the range
{tacos,nachos}	Matches one word in the list

Types of wildcards

The asterisk (*) is the simplest and most helpful wildcard. The example below demonstrates using the asterisk wildcard to display all files that match a file name.

```
$ ls -l /etc/host*
-rw-r--r-- 1 root root  92 2008-12-23 12:53 /etc/host.conf
-rw-r--r-- 1 root root   6 2009-04-23 15:50 /etc/hostname
-rw-r--r-- 1 root root 251 2009-05-22 14:55 /etc/hosts
-rw-r--r-- 1 root root 579 2009-04-20 09:14 /etc/hosts.allow
-rw-r--r-- 1 root root 878 2009-04-20 09:14 /etc/hosts.deny
```

Listing files using the asterisk wildcard

Typing `ls -l /etc/host*` lists all the files in the `/etc` directory that start with the word *host*. Other examples of wildcards are demonstrated below.

```
$ ls -l /etc/hosts.{allow,deny}
-rw-r--r-- 1 root root 579 2009-04-20 09:14 /etc/hosts.allow
-rw-r--r-- 1 root root 878 2009-04-20 09:14 /etc/hosts.deny
$ ls -l /etc/hosts.[!a]*
-rw-r--r-- 1 root root 878 2009-04-20 09:14 /etc/hosts.deny
$ ls -l /etc/host?
-rw-r--r-- 1 root root 251 2009-05-22 14:55 /etc/hosts
```

Examples of other wildcards

In this example, the first command uses `{allow,deny}` to display all matches that end with the word allow or deny. The second command uses `[!a]*` to display matches that do not begin with the letter *a* (after the period). The third example uses the `?` wildcard to match only a single character.

Pipes

Pipes (also referred to as pipelines) can be used to direct the output of one command to the input of another. Pipes are executed using the | key (usually located above the backslash key) on the keyboard.

```
$ ls -l /etc | more
total 968
-rw-r--r-- 1 root root        2975 2008-08-18 13:30 adduser.conf
-rw-r--r-- 1 root root          44 2010-04-06 16:59 adjtime
-rw-r--r-- 1 root root          51 2008-08-18 13:49 aliases
-rw-r--r-- 1 root root       12288 2009-08-28 13:39 aliases.db
drwxr-xr-x 2 root root        4096 2010-04-05 10:59 alternatives
drwxr-xr-x 7 root root        4096 2010-04-05 10:59 apache2
drwxr-xr-x 3 root root        4096 2008-08-18 13:48 apm
drwxr-xr-x 2 root root        4096 2009-08-28 13:39 apparmor
drwxr-xr-x 6 root root        4096 2008-08-18 13:47 apparmor.d
drwxr-xr-x 4 root root        4096 2010-01-25 13:44 apt
-rw-r----- 1 root daemon       144 2007-02-20 07:41 at.deny
-rw-r--r-- 1 root root        1733 2008-05-12 13:33 bash.bashrc
-rw-r--r-- 1 root root      216529 2008-04-14 20:45 bash_completion
drwxr-xr-x 2 root root        4096 2010-04-05 10:59 bash_completion.d
:
```

Using pipes on the command line

Using `ls -l` on the /etc directory would normally rapidly scroll the contents of the directory across the screen. Piping the output of `ls -l` to the **more** command (discussed on page 78) displays the contents of the /etc directory one page at a time.

Another command commonly used with pipes is **grep** (discussed on page 83). The **grep** utility can be used to filter the output of a command or file and display matching results. The next example demonstrates piping the output of the `ls` command to **grep** to filter the results and display matches that contain the word *hosts*.

```
$ ls -l /etc | grep host
-rw-r--r-- 1 root root          92 2007-10-20 06:51 host.conf
-rw-r--r-- 1 root root           9 2008-08-19 15:29 hostname
-rw-r--r-- 1 root root         300 2009-12-07 09:19 hosts
-rw-r--r-- 1 root root         579 2008-08-18 13:30 hosts.allow
-rw-r--r-- 1 root root         878 2008-08-18 13:30 hosts.deny
```

Using a pipe with the grep command to filter a command's output

Note	*Pipes are extremely useful when working on the command line. From this point on they will be appearing frequently in examples.*

Redirection

The output of a command can be redirected to other locations such as a text file. Redirection is initiated by using the > character on the keyboard.

```
$ date > date.txt
$ ls -l date.txt
-rw-r--r-- 1 nick nick 29 2009-06-10 11:37 date.txt
```
Redirecting the output of the date command to a file

In the above example, the **date** command's output is redirected to a file called date.txt instead of being displayed on the screen. If the specified file does not exist it will automatically be created. If it does exist, it will be overwritten. To prevent overwriting a file you can use >> to append to the file as shown in the next example.

```
$ date >> date.txt
```
Appending the output of a command to a file

There are two different types of output:

       1. Standard output (STDOUT)
       2. Error output (STDERR)

STDOUT and *STDERR* can be selectively directed to specific files. This is useful when trying to capture error messages as demonstrated below.

```
$ ls -l /NonExistantFile 1>ls.txt 2>lserror.txt
$ ls -l ls*
-rw-r--r-- 1 nick nick 61 2009-06-10 11:46 lserror.txt
-rw-r--r-- 1 nick nick  0 2009-06-10 11:46 ls.txt
```
Selectively redirecting STDOUT and STDERR

In this example, 1> represents *STDOUT* and 2> is for *STDERR*. Since the requested file does not exist, an error message is logged in the lserror.txt file. All non-error output is saved in the ls.txt file.

In addition to *STDOUT* and *STDERR* you can also redirect input from another location (such as a file) to a command. This is known as standard input or *STDIN*. The next example demonstrates using *STDIN* to feed the contents of a file to the **mail** command (discussed on page 173).

```
$ mail grepnick@gmail.com < ShoppingList.txt
```
Redirecting input from a file to a command

mv

Purpose: Move or rename files and directories.

Usage syntax: mv [OPTIONS] [SOURCE] [DESTINATION]

```
$ ls -l
-rw-r--r-- 1 nick nick    55 2009-05-20 15:32 MyFile
$ mv MyFile MyFile.old
$ ls -l
-rw-r--r-- 1 nick nick    55 2009-05-20 15:32 MyFile.old
```

Using the mv command to rename a file

The **mv** command moves or renames files. In the above example, MyFile file is renamed to MyFile.old using the **mv** command. In the next example, MyFile.old is moved to the /tmp directory.

```
$ mv MyFile.old /tmp/
$ ls -l /tmp/
-rw-r--r-- 1 nick nick    55 2009-05-20 15:32 MyFile.old
```

Moving a file to a different directory

The **mv** command can also be used to move or rename directories. In the example below, the NewFiles directory is renamed to OldFiles.

```
$ ls -ld NewFiles/
drwxr-xr-x 2 nick nick 4096 2009-06-28 13:23 NewFiles/
$ mv NewFiles/ OldFiles/
$ ls -ld OldFiles/
drwxr-xr-x 2 nick nick 4096 2009-06-28 13:23 OldFiles/
```

Moving an entire directory

Warning	The default behavior the **mv** command will overwrite any existing file(s). The -i option overrides this behavior and prompts the user before overwriting the destination file.

Common usage examples:

mv [SOURCE] [DEST]	Move a file or directory to the specified location
mv -i [SOURCE] [DEST]	Prompt before overwriting the destination file
mv -f [SOURCE] [DEST]	Force overwriting if the destination file exists

cp

Purpose: Copy files and directories.

Usage syntax: `cp [OPTIONS] [SOURCE] [DESTINATION]`

```
$ cp MyFile MyFile.copy
$ ls -l
-rw-r--r-- 1 nick nick     55 2009-05-20 15:32 MyFile
-rw-r--r-- 1 nick nick     55 2009-05-20 15:32 MyFile.copy
```
Creating a copy of a file

The `cp` command copies files and directories. In the above example, `MyFile` is copied to create the `MyFile.copy` file.

The next example demonstrates using `cp -r` to recursively copy the contents of a directory.

```
$ ls -l
drwxr-xr-x 2 root root     4096 Jul  1 14:06 MyDocuments
$ cp -r MyDocuments/ MyDocuments2/
$ ls -l
drwxr-xr-x 2 root root     4096 Jul  1 14:06 MyDocuments
drwxr-xr-x 2 root root     4096 Jul  1 14:06 MyDocuments2
```
Using the -r option with cp to recursively copy a directory

After executing the `cp -r` command an exact copy of the specified directory is created.

Warning	The default behavior the `cp` command will overwrite any existing file(s). The `-i` option overrides this behavior and prompts the user before overwriting the destination file.

Common usage examples:

cp [SOURCE] [DEST]	Create a copy of the specified file
cp -r [SOURCE] [DEST]	Recursively copy a directory
cp -i [SOURCE] [DEST]	Prompt before overwriting the destination file
cp -f [SOURCE] [DEST]	Force overwriting if the destination file exists
cp -v [SOURCE] [DEST]	Display verbose messages while copying

rm

Purpose: Remove files.

Usage syntax: rm [OPTIONS] [FILE]

```
$ rm MyFile
$ ls -l MyFile
ls: cannot access MyFile: No such file or directory
```
Using the rm command to remove a file

The **rm** command removes files. In the above example, the **rm** command is used to remove MyFile. After executing the **rm** command, MyFile is deleted from the disk and no longer accessible.

Notice that no warning is given when the file is removed. This is the default behavior of **rm** on most systems. To change this, use the **−i** option as demonstrated in the next example. This will instruct the system to prompt you to verify you want to remove the file.

```
$ rm -i MyFile
rm: remove regular file 'MyFile'? y
```
Using the -i option with the rm command for interactive prompts

Tip	*You can use the* **alias** *command (see page 61) to make* **rm −i** *the default remove action. This is highly recommended as it helps prevent accidental disasters when deleting files.*

Common usage examples:

rm [FILE]	Remove the specified file
rm −r [DIRECTORY]	Recursively remove all items in the specified directory
rm −i [FILE]	Prompt to confirm the removal of the specified file

mkdir / rmdir

Purpose: Create/remove directories.

Usage syntax: mkdir [OPTIONS] [DIRECTORY]

```
# mkdir test
# ls -ld test/
drwxr-xr-x 2 root root        4096 Jun  4 09:00 test
```
Creating a directory with mkdir

The `mkdir` command creates directories. The above example demonstrates creating a directory called test. Notice the permissions section of the `ls` output contains a d prefix. This indicates that the item is a directory.

Tip	*Use* `mkdir "my directory"` *or* `mkdir my\ directory` *to create a directory with a space in its name.*

The `rmdir` command removes directories. In the next example, the `rmdir` command is used to remove the previously created test directory.

Usage syntax: rmdir [DIRECTORY]

```
$ rmdir test/
$ ls -ld test/
ls: cannot access test/: No such file or directory
```
Removing a directory using rmdir

Note	`rmdir` *will only remove empty directories. To remove a non-empty directory, use* `rm -r [DIRECTORY]` *in place of the* `rmdir` *command.*

Common usage examples:

mkdir [DIRECTORY]	Create the specified directory
mkdir -p [PATH/DIRECTORY]	Create parent directories if needed
rmdir [DIRECTORY]	Remove the specified directory

touch

Purpose: Update time stamps on a file.

Usage syntax: touch [OPTIONS] [FILE]

```
$ ls -l testfile
-rw-r--r-- 1 root root 251 2009-04-21 15:50 testfile
$ touch testfile
$ ls -l testfile
-rw-r--r-- 1 root root 251 2009-05-23 14:54 testfile
$ date
Sat May 23 14:54:35 CDT 2009
```

Using the touch command to update the time stamp on a file

The touch command updates the time stamps on the specified file(s). Notice the timestamp on the file in the above example is updated to match the current time and date after executing the touch command.

If the file does not exist, the touch command will create an empty file with the specified file name, as demonstrated in the next example.

```
$ ls -l MyFile
ls: cannot access MyFile: No such file or directory
$ touch MyFile
$ ls -l MyFile
-rw-r--r-- 1 nick nick 0 2009-05-23 14:54 MyFile
```

Creating a new empty file with the the touch command

Common usage examples:

touch [FILE]	Update the time stamp on the specified file
touch -a [FILE]	Update the access time stamp on the specified file
touch -m [FILE]	Update the modified time stamp on the specified file

lsof

Purpose: List open files.

Usage syntax: lsof [OPTIONS] [NAME]

```
# lsof /etc/hosts
COMMAND    PID   USER    FD   TYPE DEVICE SIZE     NODE NAME
tail     12793 nick     3r   REG    8,1  256 1777676 /etc/hosts
```

Using the lsof command to display information about an open file

The lsof command displays information about open files. Executing the lsof command with no arguments will display all open files on the system. Specifying the name of an open file will display information about who is using the file. In the example above, lsof displays which user is using the /etc/hosts file along with other helpful information such as the command name and PID number.

The -u option allows you to see all files open by the specified user as displayed in the next example.

```
# lsof -u nick
COMMAND    PID   USER    FD   TYPE DEVICE   SIZE  NODE NAME
sshd     17899 nick     cwd   DIR    8,1   4096     2 /
sshd     17899 nick     rtd   DIR    8,1   4096     2 /
tail     12793 nick      3r   REG    8,1    256 1777676 /etc/hosts
sshd     17899 nick      0u   CHR    1,3          5818 /dev/null
sshd     17899 nick      1u   CHR    1,3          5818 /dev/null
sshd     17899 nick      2u   CHR    1,3          5818 /dev/null
...
```

Using the lsof command to display files opened by a specific user

Common usage examples:

lsof	List all open files
lsof [FILE]	List information about a specific file
lsof -u [USERNAME]	List files open by the specified user
lsof -p [PID]	List open files by the specified PID number
lsof -c [PROCESSNAME]	List open files with the specified process name
lsof -i	List open network ports and sockets

fuser

Purpose: Display information about open files.

Usage syntax: `fuser [OPTIONS] [DIRECTORY/FILE]`

```
$ fuser -v /home/nick/ShoppingList.txt
28528c(nick)
                        USER      PID  ACCESS  COMMAND
ShoppingList.txt:       nick     14044  ..c..   tail
```

Displaying information about open files with fuser

`fuser` is a helpful program for identifying the person or program that is using a file. In the example above the `fuser` command displays the user, process id, and command currently using the `ShoppingList.txt` file.

The `-ki` option can be used with the `fuser` command to terminate the process currently using the specified file as shown in the next example.

```
$ fuser -ki /home/nick/ShoppingList.txt
/home/nick/ShoppingList.txt:              14044
Kill process 14044 ? (y/N) y
```

Using the -ki option with fuser to terminate the processes using a file

Note	*Section 6 of this guide covers processes in more detail.*

Common usage examples:

`fuser [FILE]`	Display processes using the specified file
`fuser -v [FILE]`	Display detailed information about the file in use
`fuser -ki [FILE]`	Kill all processes using the specified file

cksum

Purpose: Display the checksum of a file.

Usage syntax: cksum [OPTIONS] [FILE]

```
$ cksum ubuntu.iso
3212199805 730554368 ubuntu.iso
```

Displaying the checksum of a large file

The **cksum** command displays the checksum of the specified file. It is typically used to verify the integrity of files transferred across a network connection. In the above example, the checksum for a downloaded Ubuntu Linux CD image is displayed. The resulting checksum can be compared to the checksum from the original file to ensure it arrived without errors.

The table below describes the output fields of the **cksum** command.

Checksum	File Size	File Name
3212199805	730554368	ubuntu.iso

Output fields of the cksum command

Tip	Multiple files can be analyzed with one invocation of the **cksum** command using the following syntax: **cksum [FILE1] [FILE2] [FILE3] [ETC]**.

Common usage examples:

cksum [FILE]   │ Display the checksum of the specified file(s)

md5sum

Purpose: Display the MD5 hash of a file.

Usage syntax: md5sum [OPTIONS] [FILE]

```
$ md5sum ubuntu.iso
cace6ea9dde8dc158174e345aabe3fae  ubuntu.iso
```
Displaying the md5 hash of a large file using the md5sum command

The md5sum command computes the MD5 sum (sometimes referred to as the *hash*) of the specified file. It is similar to the previously discussed cksum command except more intensive. MD5 hashes are the equivalent of a digital fingerprint and are not likely to be duplicated or padded in the same way that cksum hashes (in some rare instances) can.

The above example displays the MD5 hash for a Ubuntu Linux CD image downloaded from the internet. The resulting MD5 hash can be compared to the hash from the download site to ensure it arrived without errors.

Note	*The* md5 *command is used on BSD systems in place of* md5sum.

Common usage examples:

md5sum [FILE]	Compute the MD5 sum for the specified file(s)
md5sum -c [FILE]	Compare the MD5 sum in the specified file

ln

Purpose: Create links (shortcuts) to files or directories.

Usage syntax: `ln [OPTIONS] [TARGET] [LINK]`

```
$ ln -s TheSourceFile ThisIsTheLink
$ ls -l
-rw-r--r-- 1 nick nick 14 2009-05-23 10:16 TheSourceFile
lrwxrwxrwx 1 nick nick 13 2009-05-23 10:18 ThisIsTheLink -> TheSourceFile
```
Creating a link to a file using the ln command

The `ln` command creates links to files or directories. A link is the command line equivalent of a shortcut. In the above example, a link to a file called `TheSourceFile` is created. Notice the link in the above example has an `l` prefix in the permissions section. This indicates that the file is a link.

The default operation of the `ln` command on most systems creates what is known as a hard link. Hard links have two major limitations:

1. Hard links cannot refer to directories
2. Hard links cannot span multiple file systems/disks

Symbolic links are more commonly used today to overcome the shortfalls of hard links. They are created when using the `-s` option with the `ln` command. This is the recommended way to create a link as it will not suffer from the same limitations of a hard link.

Note	*Editing a symbolic link file is the same as editing the source file, but deleting the symbolic link does not delete the source file.*

Common usage examples:

`ln [SOURCE] [TARGET]`	Create a hard link to the specified target
`ln -s [SOURCE] [TARGET]`	Create a symbolic link to the specified target

alias

Purpose: Create command line aliases.

Usage syntax: `alias [OPTIONS] [COMMAND]`

```
$ alias rm="rm -i"
$ rm TestFile
rm: remove regular empty file 'TestFile'? y
```
Creating a command alias

The `alias` command creates command line aliases. This allows you to abbreviate a long command string to something simple. In the above example, the `rm` command is aliased to be `rm -i` so that every time the `rm` command is executed the `-i` option is automatically included (without having to type it).

Executing `alias` with no arguments will display all currently defined aliases, as demonstrated in the next example.

```
$ alias
alias cp='cp -i'
alias l='ls -l'
alias rm='rm -i'
```
Displaying all defined aliases

Tip	*Aliases are lost when you log out. The* `unalias` *command can be used to delete aliases without having to logoff. To make an alias permanent you must add it to* `/etc/profile` *or* `.*profile` *file in the user's home directory.*

Common usage examples:

`alias`	Display defined aliases
`alias [NAME]="[COMMAND]"`	Create an alias for the specified command

gzip / gunzip

Purpose: Compress/uncompress files.

Usage syntax: `gzip [OPTIONS] [FILE]`

```
# ls -lh BigFile
-rw-r--r-- 1 root root 3.0M 2010-05-20 14:02 BigFile
# gzip BigFile
# ls -lh BigFile.gz
-rw-r--r-- 1 root root 433K 2010-05-20 14:02 BigFile.gz
```

Using gzip to compress a file

`gzip` is a simple compression utility found on most Linux and BSD systems. In the above example `gzip` is used to reduce the size of the `BigFile` file by compressing it into a `.gz` archive.

The `gunzip` (or `gzip -d`) command uncompresses `gzip` archives as demonstrated in the next example.

Usage syntax: `gunzip [OPTIONS] [FILE]`

```
$ gunzip BigFile.gz
# ls -lh BigFile
-rw-r--r-- 1 root root 3.0M 2010-05-20 14:02 BigFile
```

Uncompressing a file with gunzip

Note	On older Unix systems the **compress** and **uncompress** commands are used in place of `gzip` and `gunzip`. Compressed files on these systems will usually have a `.Z` file extension in place of `.gz`.

Common usage examples:

`gzip [FILE]`	Compress the specified file
`gzip --fast [FILE]`	Compress the specified file using the fastest method
`gzip --best [FILE]`	Compress the file using the highest compression level
`gzip -tv [ARCHIVE]`	Test the specified archive for errors
`gzip -l [ARCHIVE]`	Display information about the specified archive file
`gunzip [ARCHIVE]`	Uncompress the specified archive
`gzip -d [ARCHIVE]`	Uncompress the specified archive

split

Purpose: Split large files into multiple pieces.

Usage syntax: `split [OPTIONS] [FILE] [OUTPUT]`

```
$ ls -l ubuntu.iso
-rw-r--r-- 1 nick nick 671686656 2009-10-27 12:07 ubuntu-9.10.iso
$ split -d -b 100M ubuntu.iso ubuntu.iso.
$ ls -lh ubuntu*
-rw-r--r-- 1 nick nick 641M 2009-10-27 12:07 ubuntu-9.10.iso
-rw-r--r-- 1 nick nick 100M 2010-04-11 11:44 ubuntu.iso.00
-rw-r--r-- 1 nick nick 100M 2010-04-11 11:44 ubuntu.iso.01
-rw-r--r-- 1 nick nick 100M 2010-04-11 11:44 ubuntu.iso.02
-rw-r--r-- 1 nick nick 100M 2010-04-11 11:44 ubuntu.iso.03
-rw-r--r-- 1 nick nick 100M 2010-04-11 11:44 ubuntu.iso.04
-rw-r--r-- 1 nick nick 100M 2010-04-11 11:44 ubuntu.iso.05
-rw-r--r-- 1 nick nick  41M 2010-04-11 11:44 ubuntu.iso.06
```
Using the split command to split a large file into multiple pieces

The `split` command splits large files into multiple pieces. The above example demonstrates splitting the large `ubuntu.iso` file into several 100MB pieces (as specified by the `-b 100M` parameter). In this example, the `split` command will create the required number of 100MB files with an incrementing extension.

> **Note** *The original file is left in place when creating split files.*

The `cat` command (discussed on page 75) can be used to rejoin the split files as demonstrated in the next example.

```
$ cat ubuntu.iso.* > ubuntu-joined.iso
$ ls -lh *.iso
-rw-r--r-- 1 nick nick 641M 2009-10-27 12:07 ubuntu-9.10.iso
-rw-r--r-- 1 nick nick 641M 2010-04-11 11:47 ubuntu-joined.iso
```
Combining split files using the cat command

> **Tip** *You can use the `cksum` or `md5sum` command to verify the joined file is the same as the original.*

Common usage examples:

`split -b [SIZE] [FILE] [OUTPUT]`	Split a file into multiple pieces
`split -d -b [SIZE] [FILE] [OUTPUT]`	Use numeric suffixes

shred

Purpose: Securely erase files.

Usage syntax: `shred [OPTIONS] [DIRECTORY/FILE]`

```
$ shred -u SecretPlans.txt
$ ls -l SecretPlans.txt
ls: cannot access SecretPlans.txt: No such file or directory
```
Using the shred command to securely overwrite a file

The **shred** command securely overwrites (and optionally deletes) files. In the above example, executing **shred -u** securely overwrites and removes the `SecretPlans.txt` file from the disk.

The default operation of the **shred** command overwrites the specified file with 3 passes of random data. The **-n** option can be used to specify a custom number of overwrite iterations as displayed in the next example.

```
$ shred -n 10 -v SecretPlans.txt
shred: SecretPlans.txt: pass 1/10 (random)...
shred: SecretPlans.txt: pass 2/10 (ffffff)...
shred: SecretPlans.txt: pass 3/10 (000000)...
shred: SecretPlans.txt: pass 4/10 (333333)...
shred: SecretPlans.txt: pass 5/10 (555555)...
shred: SecretPlans.txt: pass 6/10 (random)...
shred: SecretPlans.txt: pass 7/10 (aaaaaa)...
shred: SecretPlans.txt: pass 8/10 (924924)...
shred: SecretPlans.txt: pass 9/10 (492492)...
shred: SecretPlans.txt: pass 10/10 (random)...
```
Specifying a number of overwrite iterations

Note	The **-v** option is applied in the above example to verbosely display the progress of the **shred** command.

Common usage examples:

shred [FILE]	Shred the specified file
shred -u [FILE]	Shred and delete the specified file
shred -zu [FILE]	Attempt to hide evidence of file shredding
shred -v [FILE]	Display the progress of each pass
shred -n [NUM] [FILE]	Perform the specified number of overwrite passes

watch

Purpose: Periodically execute the specified command.

Usage syntax: watch [OPTIONS] [COMMAND]

```
$ watch -n 10 who
Every 10.0s: who                                Sat May 23 11:00:19 2009
steve      tty1       2009-05-21 10:24
root       tty2       2009-05-21 10:44
nick       tty3       2009-05-23 12:20
```

Executing the who command every 10 seconds using watch

watch periodically runs the specified command. It is a helpful program for monitoring the output of a command over a period of time. In the above example, watch -n 10 is used to execute the who command (discussed on page 102) every 10 seconds.

If the -n option is omitted watch will execute the specified command with a two second interval.

> **Tip**
>
> *Press* **CTRL + C** *on your keyboard to end monitoring and exit the* watch *program.*

Common usage examples:

watch [COMMAND]	Run the specified command every 2 seconds
watch -n [NUM] [COMMAND]	Run a command at the specified interval
watch -b [COMMAND]	Beep if the command exits with an error
watch -d [COMMAND]	Highlight differences between updates

env

Purpose: Display environment variables.

Usage syntax: `env [OPTIONS]`

```
$ env
TERM=xterm
SHELL=/bin/bash
USER=nick
PATH=/usr/local/sbin:/usr/local/bin:/usr/sbin:/usr/bin:/sbin:/bin:
LANG=en_US.UTF-8
HOME=/home/nick
...
```

Output of the env command

The `env` command displays your defined environment variables. These variables hold information for common account settings like the location of a user's home directory and the type of shell they use by default.

The following table describes the most common environment variables used on Unix, Linux, and BSD systems.

Variable	Function
EDITOR	Specifies the user's preferred text editor
HISTFILE	Location of the user's command line history file
HISTFILESIZE	Specifies the number of commands to save in HISTFILE
HOME	Path to the user's home directory
LANG	Specifies the user's language locale settings
MAIL	Path to the user's mail file
PATH	Path to search for binary programs
PS1	Customized shell prompt settings
SHELL	Location of the user's shell
TERM	Specifies the type of terminal being used
USER	User's username

Common environment variables used on Unix, Linux, and BSD systems

Common usage examples:

`env` | Display all defined environment variables

Section 4:
Text Editing and Extraction

Overview

Extracting and editing text is an important part of working on the command line. Text editors and utilities are commonly used for administrative purposes such as changing settings in configuration files or viewing system log files. This chapter provides a basic overview of working with text editing and extraction programs for Unix, Linux, and BSD systems.

Commands covered in this section:

Command	Purpose
nano	Simple text editor.
vi/vim	Full featured text editor.
emacs	Robust and extensible text editor.
sed	Complex stream editor.
awk	Text processing and pattern matching program.
strings	Extract readable characters from binary files.
cat	Concatenate files and display their contents.
tac	Concatenate files in reverse order.
wc	Count the number of lines, words, and characters in a file.
more	Display the output of a command or text file one page at a time.
less	Display the output of a command or text file one page (or line) at a time.
head	Display the first part of a file.
tail	Display the last part of a file.
tee	Display the output of a command and write the output to a file.
grep	Match patterns and filter data.
sort	Sort the contents of an input stream or file.
zcat	Read the contents of a compressed file.
diff	Compare files.
dostounix unixtodos	Convert text file formats between Windows/DOS and Unix/Linux systems.

Glossary of terms used in this section:

Editor	A program used to create/edit text documents.
Concatenate	Process used to join files.
Regular Expression	A complex pattern matching language.
Stream	A channel of data to/from another program or file.

nano

Purpose: Simple text editor.

Usage syntax: `nano [OPTIONS] [FILE]`

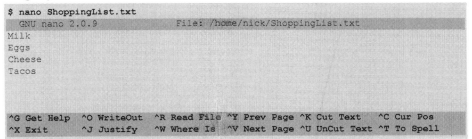

```
$ nano ShoppingList.txt
  GNU nano 2.0.9              File: /home/nick/ShoppingList.txt
Milk
Eggs
Cheese
Tacos



^G Get Help  ^O WriteOut   ^R Read File ^Y Prev Page ^K Cut Text    ^C Cur Pos
^X Exit      ^J Justify    ^W Where Is  ^V Next Page ^U UnCut Text  ^T To Spell
```

Editing a text file with nano

nano is a simple editor found on most Linux and BSD systems. It is the recommended editor for new users. Nano's functions such as searching, saving, and closing files are controlled using function keys. The basic functions are listed at the bottom of the **nano** screen. For example, pressing **CTRL + O** saves the changes to a file and **CTRL + X** exits the **nano** editor. Other functions are described in the following table.

Keys	Function	Keys	Function
CTRL + O	Save	**CTRL + X**	Exit
CTRL + G	Help	**ESC + X**	Toggle menu display
Page Up	Previous page	**Page Down**	Next Page
ESC + D	Display word count	**CTRL + C**	Display current position
CTRL + K	Cut current line	**ESC + 6**	Copy current line
CTRL + U	Paste	**CTRL + **	Find and replace
CTRL + W	Search	**CTRL + -**	Go to line
CTRL + A	Go to beginning of line	**CTRL + E**	Go to end of line
**ESC + **	Go to first line of the file	**ESC + /**	Go to last line of the file

Function keys for the nano editor

> **Note** *On some systems the* `pico` *editor may be used in place of* **nano**.

Common usage examples:

`nano [FILE]`	Open the specified file for editing
`nano -v [FILE]`	Open the specified file in read only mode

vi / vim

Purpose: Full featured text editor.

Usage syntax: `vi/vim [OPTIONS] [FILE]`

```
$ vim ShoppingList.txt
Milk
Eggs
Cheese
Tacos
~
~
~
~
~
"/home/nick/ShoppingList.txt" 4 lines, 19 characters
```

Using vi to edit a text file

The `vi` editor (also known as `vim`) is a complex and full featured text editor for Unix, Linux, and BSD systems. Traditional Unix systems typically utilize `vi` as the default text editor. Modern Linux and BSD systems use `vim` which is an enhanced version of `vi`.

The `vi` and `vim` editors have two basic modes of operation: *command mode* and *editing mode*. Pressing **Esc** on the keyboard activates command mode. When in command mode, command keys can be used to activate specific editing functions. The following table lists the most common commands for `vi` and `vim`.

Key(s)	Function	Key(s)	Function
`:w`	Save	`A`	Append text after
`:x`	Save and exit	`r`	Replace text before cursor
`:q`	Quit	`R`	Replace text after cursor
`i`	Insert text before	`yy`	Copy current line
`I`	Insert text after	`p`	Paste copied text
`a`	Append text before	`/[TEXT]`	Search for the specified text

Command keys for vi and vim

Common usage examples:

`vi [FILE]`	Open the specified file for editing in vi
`vim [FILE]`	Open the specified file for editing in vim
`view [FILE]`	Open the specified file in read only mode

emacs

Purpose: Robust and extensible text editor.

Usage syntax: emacs [OPTIONS] [FILE]

```
$ emacs ShoppingList.txt
File Edit Options Buffers Tools Help
Milk
Eggs
Cheese
Tacos




--u-:%%-F1  ShoppingList.txt (Fundamental)--L12--Top--------------------
Buffer is read-only: #<buffer services>
```

Editing a text file with emacs

emacs is one of the oldest text editors still in use today on Unix, Linux, and BSD systems. Its programmable macros and code syntax highlighting make it a popular choice for software developers and web programmers. The screenshot above displays the emacs editor user interface.

> **Note** emacs *is an incredibly powerful editor geared towards advanced users, software developers, and publishers. New users should focus on learning the* nano *and* vi *editors before attempting to master* emacs.

Common usage examples:

emacs [FILE] | Open the specified file for editing.

sed

Purpose: Complex stream editor.

Usage syntax: `sed [OPTIONS] [FILE]`

```
$ cat ShoppingList.txt
Milk
Eggs
Cheese
Tacos
$ sed s/Tacos/Nachos/ ShoppingList.txt > NewShoppingList.txt
$ cat NewShoppingList.txt
Milk
Eggs
Cheese
Nachos
```

Using the sed command to replace text in a file

sed is a complex stream editor. It uses regular expressions to modify data streamed to it. Regular expressions are a pattern matching language supported on all Unix, Linux, and BSD systems.

In the above example, the **sed** command reads the contents of the ShoppnigList.txt file and uses a regular expression to replace all instances of the word *Tacos* with *Nachos*. The results are output to a new file called NewShoppingList.txt.

Note	*Regular expressions are complex and can't be fully covered in this book. Visit www.DontFearTheCommandLine.com to find resources for learning more about regular expressions syntax.*

Common usage examples:

`sed [OPTIONS] [EXPRESSION] [FILE]` | Edit a file using sed

awk

Purpose: Text processing and pattern matching program.

Usage syntax: `awk [EXPRESSION]`

```
$ ls -l ShoppingList.*
-rw-r--r-- 1 nick nick 24 2010-04-12 23:10 ShoppingList.old
-rw-r--r-- 1 nick nick 23 2010-04-12 19:33 ShoppingList.txt
$ ls -l ShoppingList.* | awk  -F" " '{ print $1 " " $8 }'
-rw-r--r-- ShoppingList.old
-rw-r--r-- ShoppingList.txt
```

Modifying the output of the ls command using the awk command

`awk` is a pattern matching and text processing utility. It treats each line of input as a series of fields. The fields in each line are grouped into an array and assigned a variable related to their position. In the above example, `awk` is used to extract and print the first and eighth (`$1` and `$8`) fields from the output of the `ls` command.

The `awk` command can also be used to perform batch processing functions such as renaming multiple files as demonstrated in the next example.

```
$ ls
File1   File3   File5   File7   File9
File2   File4   File6   File8
$ ls | awk '{print "mv "$1" "$1".txt"}' | sh
$ ls
File1.txt   File3.txt   File5.txt   File7.txt   File9.txt
File2.txt   File4.txt   File6.txt   File8.txt
```

Batch renaming files using the awk command

In this example the `awk` command is used to rename the listed files by appending a `.txt` extension to them.

Note	*awk is a powerful and complex utility that can't be fully covered in this book. Visit www.DontFearTheCommandLine.com to find resources for learning more about* `awk` *usage syntax.*

Common usage examples:

`[INPUT] | awk [EXPRESSION]` | Process input using the awk command

strings

Purpose: Extract readable characters from binary files.

Usage syntax: `strings [OPTIONS] [FILE]`

```
$ strings unknown.mp3
...
TAG Girl You Know It's True
Milli Vanilli
Girl You Know It's True
1989
...
```

Using the strings command to extract text from a binary file

The `strings` command extracts text from binary files. Binary files contain data that is unreadable using standard text processing programs. Examples of binary files include MP3, JPEG, and MPEG to name a few.

In the above example, readable text is extracted from the `unknown.mp3` file. This information can be used to identify the contents of the binary file.

Note	*The `strings` command displays results that are a minimum of 4 characters by default. You can override the default minimum character length using the `-n` option.*

Common usage examples:

`strings [FILE]`	Display readable text characters in a binary file
`strings -n [NUM] [FILE]`	Set the minimum number of characters

cat

Purpose: Concatenate files and display their contents.

Usage syntax: cat [OPTIONS] [FILE]

```
$ cat ShoppingList.txt
Milk
Eggs
Cheese
Tacos
```

Output of the cat command

The cat command concatenates and displays files. Executing cat on the ShoppingList.txt file displays its contents as shown in the above example.

To join two or more files, simply provide the file names to be concatenated separated by a space as demonstrated in the next example.

```
$ cat ShoppingList.txt NachoIngredients.txt
Milk
Eggs
Cheese
Tacos
2 cloves garlic, crushed
6 green onions, sliced, white parts and tops separated
1 cup salsa
1/2 (12 ounce) package tortilla chips
1 (8 ounce) package shredded Cheddar/Monterey Jack cheese blend
1/2 large tomato, diced
```

Joining two files using the cat command

Common usage examples:

cat [FILE]	Display the contents of the specified file
cat [FILE1] [FILE2] [ETC]	Join the specified files
cat -n [FILE]	Display numbered output for each line
cat -s [FILE]	Suppress blank lines

tac

Purpose: Concatenate files in reverse order.

Usage syntax: `tac [FILE]`

```
$ cat ShoppingList.txt
Milk
Eggs
Cheese
Tacos
$ tac ShoppingList.txt
Tacos
Cheese
Eggs
Milk
```

Comparison of the output from the cat and tac commands

The `tac` command is similar to the previously discussed `cat` command, except it displays a file's contents in reverse order. In the above example, the output of the `cat` command is compared to the `tac` command to demonstrate the differences between the output generated by these two commands.

Tip	*tac is extremely useful when reviewing the contents of log files on Unix, Linux, BSD systems. The newest entries in log files are always appended to the end of the file. tac allows you to read these files in reverse order displaying the most recent entries first.*

Common usage examples:

`tac [FILE]` | Display the contents of the specified file in reverse order

wc

Purpose: Count the number of lines, words, and characters in a file.

Usage syntax: wc [OPTIONS] [FILE]

```
$ wc /etc/hosts
10 28 251 /etc/hosts
```

Output of the wc command

The **wc** command (short for **W**ord **C**ount) displays the total number of lines, words, and characters in the specified file. The above example displays the totals for the /etc/host file. The table below explains the output fields generated by the **wc** command.

Lines	Words	Characters	File
10	28	251	/etc/hosts

Output fields of the wc command

Common usage examples:

wc [FILE]	Display the number of lines, words, and characters in a file
wc -w [FILE]	Display the number of words in a file
wc -l [FILE]	Display the number of lines in a file
wc -c [FILE]	Display the number of characters in a file

more

Purpose: Display the output of a command or text file one page at a time.

Usage syntax: `more [OPTIONS] [FILE]`

```
$ more /var/log/syslog
May 20 11:49:15 e6400 NetworkManager:      SCPlugin-Ifupdown: (19599648)
... get_connections (managed=false): return empty list.
May 20 11:49:15 e6400 modem-manager: Loaded plugin Longcheer
May 20 11:49:15 e6400 modem-manager: Loaded plugin Option
May 20 11:49:15 e6400 modem-manager: Loaded plugin MotoC
May 20 11:49:15 e6400 modem-manager: Loaded plugin Option High-Speed
May 20 11:49:15 e6400 modem-manager: Loaded plugin Generic
May 20 11:49:15 e6400 modem-manager: Loaded plugin Gobi
May 20 11:49:15 e6400 modem-manager: Loaded plugin Nokia
May 20 11:49:15 e6400 modem-manager: Loaded plugin Novatel
May 20 11:49:15 e6400 modem-manager: Loaded plugin AnyData
May 20 11:49:15 e6400 modem-manager: Loaded plugin Huawei
May 20 11:49:15 e6400 modem-manager: Loaded plugin ZTE
May 20 11:49:15 e6400 modem-manager: Loaded plugin Sierra
May 20 11:49:15 e6400 modem-manager: Loaded plugin Ericsson MBM
--More--(14%)
```

Viewing a text file with the more command

The **more** command displays the output of a command or text file one page at a time. This is useful for large files or commands that generate many lines of output. The above example demonstrates using the **more** command to read a large text file one page at a time.

> **Tip**
> *The space bar is used to scroll output using* **more**. *The* **Q** *key closes the file without having to scroll to the end.*

Common usage examples:

`more [FILE]`	Display the specified file one page at a time
`more +[NUM] [FILE]`	Start reading a file at the specified line number
`[COMMAND] | more`	Display a command's output one page at a time

less

Purpose: Display the output of a command or text file one page (or line) at a time.

Usage syntax: `less [OPTIONS] [FILE]`

```
$ less /var/log/syslog
May 20 11:49:15 e6400 NetworkManager:     SCPlugin-Ifupdown: (19599648)
... get_connections (managed=false): return empty list.
May 20 11:49:15 e6400 modem-manager: Loaded plugin Longcheer
May 20 11:49:15 e6400 modem-manager: Loaded plugin Option
May 20 11:49:15 e6400 modem-manager: Loaded plugin MotoC
May 20 11:49:15 e6400 modem-manager: Loaded plugin Option High-Speed
May 20 11:49:15 e6400 modem-manager: Loaded plugin Generic
May 20 11:49:15 e6400 modem-manager: Loaded plugin Gobi
May 20 11:49:15 e6400 modem-manager: Loaded plugin Nokia
May 20 11:49:15 e6400 modem-manager: Loaded plugin Novatel
May 20 11:49:15 e6400 modem-manager: Loaded plugin AnyData
May 20 11:49:15 e6400 modem-manager: Loaded plugin Huawei
May 20 11:49:15 e6400 modem-manager: Loaded plugin ZTE
May 20 11:49:15 e6400 modem-manager: Loaded plugin Sierra
May 20 11:49:15 e6400 modem-manager: Loaded plugin Ericsson MBM
:
```

Viewing a text file with the less command

The **less** command is similar to the previously discussed **more** command except it supports scrolling in both directions (up and down) where **more** can only go down.

Tip	*The arrow keys and* **Page Up/Down** *keys are used to scroll output using* **less**. *The* **Q** *key closes the file without having to scroll to the end.*

Common usage examples:

`less [FILE]`	Display the specified file one page at a time
`less +[NUM] [FILE]`	Start reading a file at the specified line number
`[COMMAND]	less`	Display a command's output one page at a time

head

Purpose: Display the first part of a file.

Usage syntax: head [OPTIONS] [FILE]

```
$ head -n 2 ShoppingList.txt
Milk
Eggs
```

Using the head command to display the first two lines of a file

The **head** command displays the first few lines (known as the *head*) of the specified file. In the above example, the **-n 2** option is used to display only the first two lines of the specified file. If the **head** command is executed with no options it will display the first 10 lines in the file by default.

Common usage examples:

head [FILE]	Display the first 10 lines of the specified file
head -n [NUM] [FILE]	Display the specified number of lines

tail

Purpose: Display the last part of a file.

Usage syntax: `tail [OPTIONS] [FILE]`

```
$ tail -n 2 ShoppingList.txt
Cheese
Tacos
```

Displaying the last two lines in a file with tail

The `tail` command displays the last few lines (known as the *tail*) of the specified file. In the above example, the `-n 2` option is used to display only the last two lines of the specified file. If the `tail` command is executed with no options it will display the last 10 lines in the file by default.

Another useful feature of the `tail` command is the `-f` option which is used to "follow" a file as it grows. This instructs the `tail` command to open the specified file and display new lines as they are written to it. The next example demonstrates using the `tail -f` command to monitor new log entries in real-time in the `/var/log/syslog` file.

```
# tail -f /var/log/syslog
May 22 13:41:50 e6400 NetworkManager: <info>  (wlan0): supplicant
connection state:  completed -> group handshake
May 22 13:41:50 e6400 NetworkManager: <info>  (wlan0): supplicant
connection state:  group handshake -> completed
May 22 13:41:51 e6400 wpa_supplicant[848]: WPA: EAPOL-Key Replay
Counter did not increase - dropping packet
May 22 13:41:51 e6400 wpa_supplicant[848]: WPA: Invalid EAPOL-Key MIC -
dropping packet
May 22 13:42:15 e6400 wpa_supplicant[848]: last message repeated 6
times
May 22 13:45:13 e6400 anacron[1290]: Job 'cron.daily' started
May 22 13:45:13 e6400 anacron[2167]: Updated timestamp for job
'cron.daily' to 2010-05-22
...
```

Using the tail command to monitor a growing log file in real time

Common usage examples:

`tail [FILE]`	Display the last 10 lines of the specified file
`tail -n [NUM] [FILE]`	Display the specified number of lines
`tail -f [FILE]`	Follow the file as it grows

tee

Purpose: Display the output of a command and write the output to a file.

Usage syntax: `tee [OPTIONS] [FILE]`

```
$ ls -l /etc/ | tee etc.txt
-rw-r--r-- 1 root root     2975 2009-02-04 11:12 adduser.conf
-rw-r--r-- 1 root root       46 2010-06-27 16:53 adjtime
-rw-r--r-- 1 root root      532 2009-11-30 14:33 aliases
-rw-r--r-- 1 root root    12288 2010-07-01 12:23 aliases.db
drwxr-xr-x 2 root root     4096 2010-05-04 13:24 alternatives
drwxr-xr-x 4 root root     4096 2009-03-12 14:08 amavis
drwxr-xr-x 3 root root     4096 2009-02-04 12:49 apm
drwxr-xr-x 2 root root     4096 2009-08-28 14:45 apparmor
drwxr-xr-x 6 root root     4096 2010-06-27 16:53 apparmor.d
...
```

Using the tee command to capture the output of a command

The `tee` command displays the output of a command and also saves the output to a file. In the above example, the `tee` command displays the output of the `ls -l /etc` command while simultaneously saving the results to a file called `etc.txt` file. Viewing the `etc.txt` file shows its contents are the same as the output displayed on the command line, as demonstrated in the next example.

```
$ more etc.txt
-rw-r--r-- 1 root root     2975 2009-02-04 11:12 adduser.conf
-rw-r--r-- 1 root root       46 2010-06-27 16:53 adjtime
-rw-r--r-- 1 root root      532 2009-11-30 14:33 aliases
-rw-r--r-- 1 root root    12288 2010-07-01 12:23 aliases.db
drwxr-xr-x 2 root root     4096 2010-05-04 13:24 alternatives
drwxr-xr-x 4 root root     4096 2009-03-12 14:08 amavis
drwxr-xr-x 3 root root     4096 2009-02-04 12:49 apm
drwxr-xr-x 2 root root     4096 2009-08-28 14:45 apparmor
drwxr-xr-x 6 root root     4096 2010-06-27 16:53 apparmor.d
...
```

Viewing the contents of the output file created by the tee command

Common usage examples:

`[COMMAND]	tee [FILE]`	Save a command's output to a file
`[COMMAND]	tee -a [FILE]`	Append the output to the specified file

grep

Purpose: Match patterns and filter data.

Usage syntax: grep [OPTIONS] [FILE]

```
$ grep -i failed /var/log/syslog
Apr  4 07:52:44 kernel: [0.000000] Fast TSC calibration failed
Apr  4 07:52:44 kernel: [1.587770] PM: Resume from disk failed.
Apr  4 07:52:44 kernel: [6.252517] PM: Resume from disk failed.
Apr 11 12:11:28 init: Unable to connect to the system bus: Failed to
connect to socket /var/run/dbus/system_bus_socket: Connection refused
...
```

Using the grep command to filter a file

The **grep** command filters data from a file or command. In the above example, **grep** is used to filter the /var/log/syslog file and display matches that contain the word *failed*.

> **Tip**
> Unix, Linux, and BSD systems are case sensitive. In the above example, the -i option is used to overcome this and perform a case insensitive search.

The **grep** command can also be used to filter the output of a command. In the next example the output of the **dmesg** command (discussed on page 227) is piped to the **grep** command to only display results that contain the word *error*.

```
$ dmesg | grep -i error
[16074.400692] PM: Device 2-3 failed to resume: error -19
[20792.424537] npviewer.bin[20044]: segfault at ff9bea2c ip
00000000ff9bea2c sp 00000000ffca507c error 14
[21301.607988] npviewer.bin[24229]: segfault at ff9bea2c ip
00000000ff9bea2c sp 00000000ff83a40c error 14
...
```

Using the grep command to filter a command's output

Common usage examples:

grep [STRING] [FILE]	Display matching lines in a file
grep -c [STRING] [FILE]	Count the number of matches in a file
grep -i [STRING] [FILE]	Ignore case when matching
[COMMAND]	grep [STRING]	Filter a command's output to match a string

sort

Purpose: Sort the contents of an input stream or file.

Usage syntax: `sort [OPTIONS] [FILE]`

```
$ cat ShoppingList.txt
Milk
Eggs
Cheese
Tacos
$ sort ShoppingList.txt
Cheese
Eggs
Milk
Tacos
```

Using the sort command to sort a file

The **sort** command sorts the contents command or file. In the above example, the **sort** command is used to alphabetically sort the `ShoppingList.txt` file and display the results.

sort can also be used with pipes to sort the output of a command as shown in the next example.

```
$ ls | sort
acpi
adduser.conf
adjtime
aliases
aliases.db
alsa
alternatives
anacrontab
apache2
...
```

Using the sort command to sort the output of a command

Common usage examples:

`sort [FILE]`	Sort and display the specified file
`sort -r [FILE]`	Reverse sort the specified file
`[COMMAND]	sort`	Sort the output of the specified command

zcat

Purpose: Read the contents of a compressed file.

Usage syntax: zcat [OPTIONS] [FILE]

```
$ file ShoppingList.txt.gz
ShoppingList.txt.gz: gzip compressed data, was "ShoppingList.txt", from
Unix, last modified: Mon Apr 12 19:33:38 2010
$ zcat ShoppingList.txt.gz
Milk
Eggs
Cheese
Tacos
```

Viewing the contents of a compressed text file with the zcat command

The zcat command allows you to read the contents of a compressed text file without having to manually uncompress it first. In the above example the ShoppingList.txt.gz file is a compressed **gzip** archive. Using the traditional cat command would produce unreadable output in this scenario. The zcat command, however, allows you to view the contents of the file without having to first uncompress it.

Common usage examples:

zcat [FILE] | Read the contents of a compressed file

diff

Purpose: Compare files.

Usage syntax: `diff [OPTIONS] [FILE]`

```
$ diff ShoppingList.txt ShoppingList.old
4c4
< Tacos
---
> Nachos
```

Default output of the diff command

The `diff` command allows you to compare two text files line by line and display the differences between them. The `diff` command provides two types of output:

1. Single column (default)
2. Two column side-by-side comparison (activated with the `-y` option)

In the above example the `diff` command displays the default single column output which only shows the differences between the two files. Indicators are used to mark the differing lines:

    <   Indicates the text in the first file

    >   Indicates the text in the second file

The `-y` option can be used to display two column side-by-side output. The next example demonstrates the output generated with this option.

```
$ diff -y ShoppingList.txt ShoppingList.old
Milk                              Milk
Eggs                              Eggs
Cheese                            Cheese
Tacos                           | Nachos
```

Comparing two files with the diff command

Common usage examples:

`diff [FILE1] [FILE2]`	Compare files and display differences
`diff -y [FILE1] [FILE2]`	Compare files side by side
`diff -i [FILE1] [FILE2]`	Ignore case when comparing files

dos2unix / unix2dos

Purpose: Convert file formats between Windows/MS-DOS and Unix/Linux systems.

Usage syntax: dos2unix / unix2dos [OPTIONS] [FILE]

```
$ cat ShoppingList.txt
Milk^M
Eggs^M
Cheese^M
Tacos
$ dos2unix ShoppingList.txt
$ cat ShoppingList.txt
Milk
Eggs
Cheese
Tacos
```

Converting a Windows-formatted text file to a Unix-formatted file

Text files created in Windows and MS-DOS are formatted with line feed characters that are not compatible with Unix/Linux systems. The **dos2unix** command reformats the specified file so that is will display properly on Unix/Linux systems. In the above example, the line feed characters in the ShoppingList.txt file are converted so they will display properly on Unix-based systems.

Similar to the **dos2unix** command, **unix2dos** formats text files created on Unix/Linux systems so they can be displayed properly when transferred to Windows systems.

Tip	*Conversions are done directly to the specified file. Use the −b option to create a backup of the file before converting.*

Common usage examples:

dos2unix [FILE]	Convert a Windows text file to a Unix-formatted file
dos2unix -b [FILE]	Create a backup before converting
unix2dos [FILE]	Convert a Unix text file to a Windows-formatted file
unix2dos -b [FILE]	Create a backup before converting the file

Section 5:
Users, Groups, and Security

Overview

This chapter covers the most common commands related to users, groups, and security. It will also discuss topics like account creation/deletion, file and directory permissions, and other user/security related commands.

Commands covered in this section:

Command	Purpose
chmod	Change file and directory permissions.
chown	Change the owner of a file or directory.
chgrp	Change the group of files and directories.
umask	Display/set a user's default file creation mask.
su	Switch user accounts.
sudo	Run a single command as a different user.
id	Display information about a user's identity.
groups	Display which groups a user belongs to.
who	Display who is logged into the system.
whoami	Display the current user's identity
w	Display detailed information about users logged in to the system.
last lastb	Display the last successful/failed user logins.
lastlog	Display the most recent user login information.
finger	Display information a about user account.
passwd	Change passwords.
useradd userdel	Create/delete user accounts.
adduser deluser	Create/delete user accounts on Linux systems.
groupadd groupdel	Add/remove a group.

(Continued...)

Command	Purpose
usermod groupmod	Modify user and group account settings.
wall	Broadcast a message to all users on the system.
ulimit	Display/set system resource limits.

Glossary of terms used in this section:

GID
(**G**roup **ID**entifier) A numerical value assigned to a group in the /etc/group file.

Group
A grouping of user accounts used to simplify security and access control.

Mode
Indicator of permissions for files and directories.

Octal Notation
A numerical value used to apply permissions to files and directories.

Permissions
Settings used to control access to a file or directory.

Profile
Collection of settings assigned to a user.

Symbolic Notation
A user friendly way to display or apply permissions to files and directories.

UID
(**U**ser **ID**entifier) A numerical value assigned to a user account in the /etc/passwd file.

User Account
An account assigned to each person with login access to the local system.

Types of Accounts

There are several types of user accounts used on Unix, Linux, and BSD systems. The graphic below illustrates the user security model used on most systems.

Privileges

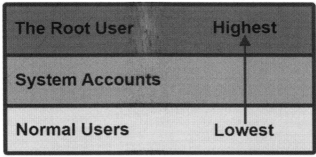

Unix/Linux/BSD user security model

By default, normal users and the programs they execute are given the least amount of privileges on the system. System accounts have slightly elevated privileges and are used to run system services (like a web server or FTP server). The root account has unrestricted administrative access to the entire system.

Groups

Groups are used to simplify the management of system security. Users can be a member of one or more groups. All users are part of at least one group by default; this group is known as the user's primary group.

File and Directory Permissions

File and directory permissions are managed using a set of nine "flags". The following example describes permissions found on a typical file.

−	rwx	r-x	r-x
	1 2 3	4 5 6	7 8 9
File Type	User (Owner)	Group	Other (Everyone)

Within these nine flags, three sets of permissions are specified:
- User (AKA owner) permissions
- Group permissions
- Other (i.e. everyone else)

There are four types of permissions that can be used to control access to a file or directory. The following table describes each permission.

Symbolic	Meaning
r	Read
w	Write
x	Execute
-	No access

Example of directory permissions

In most cases, the owner of a file will always have full read/write access to that file. Execute permission is a special flag used for programs, scripts, and directories to indicate they are executable.

The example below displays basic file permissions.

```
$ ls -l ShoppingList.txt
-rw-r--r-- 1 nick users 254 2009-06-01 15:35 ShoppingList.txt
```

Output of the ls -l command displaying file permissions

	User	Group	Other
Symbolic	rw-	r--	r--
Meaning	Read & Write	Read only	Read only

Example of file permissions

The next example demonstrates directory permissions. Directory permissions work the same as file permissions except they are used to control access to directories.

```
$ ls -ld finance/
drwxr-x--- 2 root finance 4096 2009-06-12 09:48 finance/
```

Output of the ls -ld command displaying directory permissions

	User	Group	Other
Symbolic	rwx	r-x	---
Meaning	Read, Write, & Execute	Read only & Execute	No Access

Example of directory permissions

Each file and directory has its own set of permissions. Permissions are not inherited from the parent directory. Additionally, directories require execute permission in order to be accessible, as shown in the previous example.

chmod

Purpose: Change file and directory permissions.

Usage syntax: chmod [OPTIONS] [MODE] [DIRECTORY/FILE]

```
# chmod 664 ShoppingList.txt
# ls -l ShoppingList.txt
-rw-rw-r-- 1 root root 23 2009-05-27 22:31 ShoppingList.txt
```
Using the chmod command to change file permissions

The `chmod` command sets permissions on files and directories. By default, permissions are specified in numerical (octal) format such as 664 as shown in the above example. In octal form, three digits are used to represent owner, group, and everyone else's permissions. The first number represents the owner's permissions, the second number is the group's permissions, and the third number is for everyone else.

The table below provides a cross reference of symbolic and octal permissions.

Permission	Symbolic	Octal
Read	r	4
Write	w	2
Execute	x	1
None	-	0

Permissions cross reference

The sum of the octal permissions becomes what is known as the *mode*. The valid modes are described in the following table.

Mode	Octal	Symbolic	Effective Permission
7	4+2+1	rwx	Read/Write/Execute
6	4+2	rw-	Read/Write
5	4+1	r-x	Read/Execute
4	4	r--	Read
0	0	---	None

Mode cross reference

The combination of 3 modes determines the permissions for the file. A mode of 664 would create `rw-rw-r--` permissions giving read/write access to the user and group, and read only to everyone else.

(Continued...)

The concept of permissions on Unix, Linux, and BSD systems can be hard to grasp as first. Several additional examples are provided below to help clarify this topic.

Example 1: A mode of 660 would provide read/write access to the owner and group and no access to everyone else.

```
# chmod 660 MyFile
# ls -l MyFile
-rw-rw---- 1 root sales 23 2009-05-27 22:31 MyFile
```
Result of a 660 mode

Example 2: A mode of 755 would provide full access to the owner and read/execute access for the group and everyone else.

```
# chmod 755 MyProgram.sh
# ls -l MyProgram.sh
-rwxr-xr-x 1 root sales 23 2009-05-27 22:31 MyProgram.sh
```
Result of a 755 mode

Example 3: A mode of 600 would provide read/write access to the owner and no access to everyone else.

```
# chmod 600 MyFile
# ls -l MyFile
-rw------- 1 root sales 23 2009-05-27 22:31 MyFile
```
Result of a 600 mode

Example 4: A mode of 775 applied to a directory would provide read/write/execute access to the owner and group and read only access to everyone else.

```
$ chmod 775 MyDirectory
$ ls -ld test
drwxrwxr-x 2 root sales 4096 2009-05-27 16:04 MyDirectory
```
Result of a 775 mode applied to a directory

Common usage examples:

chmod [MODE] [FILE]	Change the permissions on the specified file
chmod [MODE] -R [DIR]	Recursively change the permissions on all files

chown

Purpose: Change the owner of a file or directory.

Usage syntax: chown [OPTIONS] [USER:GROUP] [DIRECTORY/FILE]

```
# ls -l ShoppingList.txt
-rw-r--r-- 1 nick nick 23 2009-05-27 22:31 ShoppingList.txt
# chown root ShoppingList.txt
# ls -l ShoppingList.txt
-rw-r--r-- 1 root nick 23 2009-05-27 22:31 ShoppingList.txt
```

Using the chown command to change the owner of a file

The **chown** command changes the owner of a file or directory. In the above example, the owner of the ShoppingList.txt file is changed from *nick* to *root*.

The next example demonstrates changing both the owner and group of a file using the **chown** command.

```
# ls -l ShoppingList.txt
-rw-r--r-- 1 root nick 23 2009-05-27 22:31 ShoppingList.txt
# chown nick:sales ShoppingList.txt
# ls -l ShoppingList.txt
-rw-r--r-- 1 nick sales 23 2009-05-27 22:31 ShoppingList.txt
```

Using the chown command to change the owner and group of a file

After executing the **chown nick:sales ShoppingList.txt** command, the ShoppingList.txt file is updated with the owner of *nick* and the group of *sales*.

> **Tip** *You can use the* **chgrp** *command (discussed on page 96) if you only need to change the group of a file.*

Common usage examples:

chown [USER] [FILE]	Change the owner of a file
chown [USER]:[GROUP] [FILE]	Change the owner and group of a file
chown -R [USER] [DIR]	Recursively change the owner on all files in the specified directory

chgrp

Purpose: Change the group of files and directories.

Usage syntax: chgrp [OPTIONS] [GROUP] [DIRECTORY/FILE]

```
# ls -l ShoppingList.txt
-rw-r--r-- 1 root root  23 2009-05-27 22:31 ShoppingList.txt
# chgrp sales ShoppingList.txt
# ls -l ShoppingList.txt
-rw-r--r-- 1 root sales 23 2009-05-27 22:31 ShoppingList.txt
```

Using the chgrp command to change the group of a file

The chgrp command changes the group of a file or directory. In the above example the chgrp command is used to change the group from *root* to *sales* on the ShoppingList.txt file.

Common usage examples:

chgrp [GROUP] [FILE]	Change a file's group to the specified group
chgrp -R [DIR]	Recursively change the group on all files

umask

Purpose: Display/set a user's default file creation mask.

Usage syntax: umask [OPTIONS] [MODE]

```
$ umask
022
```
Displaying the current user's umask

umask controls a user's default file creation mask. This determines the permissions that will be assigned to newly created files and directories. To determine the file/directory creation mode the umask value is subtracted from 777 for directories and 666 for files. For example, a umask of 022 would create effective permissions of 644 (rw-r--r--) for files and 755 (rwxr-xr-x) for directories.

On some systems the -S option can be used to display a more user friendly symbolic output of the umask value, as shown in the next example.

```
$ umask -S
u=rwx,g=rx,o=rx
```
Displaying the umask in symbolic notation

The umask command can also be used to change the umask value as displayed in the next example.

```
$ umask 077
```
Setting the umask value

In this example, a umask value of 077 would create effective permissions of 600 (rw-------) for files and 700 (rwx------) for directories.

> **Note** *A umask value specified on the command line is reset when you log out. To make the umask permanent you must add it to the* .*profile *file in the user's home directory or* /etc/profile *(for all users).*

Common usage examples:

umask	Display the umask in octal format
umask -S	Display the umask in symbolic format
umask [MODE]	Set the umask to the specified value

su

Purpose: Switch user accounts.

Usage syntax: `su [OPTIONS] [USER]`

```
$ whoami
nick
$ su
Password: ******
# whoami
root
```
Using the su command to switch from a normal user to the root user

The `su` command (short for **S**witch **U**ser) allows you to login as another user without having to first log out of the system. In the above example `su` is used by a normal user to switch to the root user account. Notice that when you become the root user your shell prompt changes from `$` to `#`. As the root user you can now run commands that require elevated privileges.

| **Tip** | *You should always limit the amount of time you spend logged in as the root user. This is a good practice that can help reduce accidents.* |

By default, executing `su` with no arguments switches to the root user account. A user name can be specified with `su` to become a different user as shown in the next example.

```
$ whoami
nick
$ su steve
Password: ******
$ whoami
steve
```
Using su to switch to another user

Common usage examples:

`su`	Switch to the root user account
`su -`	Switch to the root user account and load root's profile
`su [USERNAME]`	Switch to the specified username

sudo

Purpose: Run a single command as a different user.

Usage syntax: `sudo [OPTIONS] [COMMAND]`

```
$ whoami
nick
$ sudo whoami
[sudo] password for nick: *******
root
$ whoami
nick
```

Using sudo to run a command as the root user

The `sudo` command allows you to run a single command as another user. It is most commonly used to execute commands that require root privileges. In this example `whoami` is executed as root via the `sudo` command.

Using the `sudo` command is the recommended way to run commands that require elevated privileges as it limits the amount of time spent with root privileges. This greatly helps prevent disasters such as accidental deletion of important system files.

> **Note** User (or group) accounts must be listed in the `/etc/sudoers` file in order to execute commands as root with `sudo`.

Common usage examples:

`sudo [COMMAND]`	Run the specified command as root
`sudo -u [USER] [COMMAND]`	Run a command as the specified user
`sudo !!`	Run the last command as root

id

Purpose: Display information about a user's identity.

Usage syntax: `id [OPTIONS] [USER]`

```
# id
uid=0(root) gid=0(root) groups=0(root)
```
Displaying user and group information for the current user

The `id` command displays user and group information for the specified user. Executing `id` with no options displays the current user's information as displayed in the above example. The next example demonstrates using the `id` command to display information about a specific user.

```
# id nick
uid=1000(nick) gid=1000(nick) groups=4(adm), 20(dialout),24(cdrom),
46(plugdev), 106(lpadmin), 121(admin), 122(sambashare), 1000(nick)
```
Displaying user and group information for a specific user

> **Note**
>
> *Unix, Linux, and BSD systems assign a numerical UID (**User ID**) and GID (**Group ID**) for each user and group on the system. A user friendly name is also assigned to each UID and GID which is displayed in parenthesis next to each ID number. This information is stored in* `/etc/passwd` *for users and* `/etc/group` *for groups.*

Common usage examples:

`id`	Display the current user's ID information
`id [USER]`	Display user and group information for the specified user

groups

Purpose: Display which groups a user belongs to.

Usage syntax: groups [OPTIONS] [USER]

```
# groups
root
```
Displaying group information for the current user

The `groups` command displays a user's group membership. Executing `groups`
with no options displays the current user's groups, as shown in the above example.
A user name can be used with the `groups` command to display the specified
user's group membership as shown in the next example.

```
# groups nick
nick adm dialout cdrom plugdev lpadmin admin sambashare
```
Displaying group information for the specified user

Common usage examples:

groups	Display the current user's group membership
groups [USER]	Display group membership for the specified user

who / whoami

Purpose: Display who is logged into the system.

Usage syntax: `who [OPTIONS]`

```
$ who
root       tty2          2010-05-17 11:32
nick       tty1          2010-05-17 11:31
nick       pts/0         2010-05-17 08:40 (10.10.1.251)
dave       pts/1         2010-05-17 12:32 (10.10.1.188)
mike       pts/2         2010-05-17 14:28 (10.10.1.167)
lisa       pts/3         2010-05-17 14:50 (10.10.1.204)
nick       pts/4         2010-05-17 15:33 (10.10.1.251)
```

Output of the who command

The `who` command displays information about users currently logged in to the system. The default output of the `who` command displays the username, terminal ID, and date/time the user logged in as shown in the above example.

Note	*Users logged in via telnet or SSH sessions will also display the IP address of the remote client in parentheses.*

The `whoami` command displays the username of the current user. This is helpful to verify which user's environment and security privileges are available when switching between different accounts.

Usage syntax: `whoami`

```
$ whoami
nick
```

Using whoami to display the name of the current user

Common usage examples:

`who`	Display who is currently logged into the system
`who -b`	Display the last system boot time
`who -r`	Display the current run level
`whoami`	Display the name of the current user

w

Purpose: Display detailed information about users logged in to the system.

Usage syntax: `w [OPTIONS] [USER]`

```
$ w
 15:39:12 up 4 days,  6:09,  5 users,  load average: 0.06, 0.05, 0.01
USER     TTY      FROM             LOGIN@   IDLE   JCPU   PCPU WHAT
nick     pts/0    10.10.1.251      08:40    1:10   0.18s  0.15s -bash
dave     pts/1    10.10.1.188      12:32    0.00s  0.14s  0.14s vim
mike     pts/2    10.10.1.167      14:28    0.00s  0.12s  0.12s tail
lisa     pts/3    10.10.1.204      14:50    9.00s  0.14s  0.14s -bash
nick     pts/4    10.10.1.251      15:33    0.00s  0.15s  0.01s w
```
Output of the w command

The `w` command shows detailed information about users logged into the system. It is similar to the previously discussed **who** command except it provides additional information such as the user's last login time, how long they have been idle, and what program they are currently running.

The `w` command also displays a system summary line that shows the host's uptime, number of connected users, and samples of system load averages for the past 1, 5, and 15 minutes.

> **Tip**
> *The information displayed on the first line is the same output generated by the* **uptime** *command. See page 226 for more information about system uptime and load averages.*

Common usage examples:

w | Display detailed information about users currently logged in to the system

last / lastb

Purpose: Display the last successful/failed user logins.

Usage syntax: `last [OPTIONS] [USER]`

```
$ last
nick      pts/1         192.168.1.50   Sat May 22 13:42   still logged in
nick      pts/0         192.168.1.50   Sat May 22 13:40   still logged in
nick      tty7          :0             Sat May 22 13:40   still logged in
reboot    system boot   2.6.32-21-ge   Sat May 22 13:40 - 14:02  (00:21)
nick      pts/0         :0.0           Thu May 20 21:33 - 21:36  (00:03)
nick      pts/0         :0.0           Thu May 20 21:30 - 21:33  (00:02)
root      pts/0         :0.0           Thu May 20 21:27 - 21:30  (00:03)
nick      tty7          :0             Thu May 20 21:25 - crash  (1+16:14)
...
```

Output of the last command

The `last` command displays the login and logout times for each user on the system. It also shows information about system shutdowns and restarts as shown in the above example.

The `lastb` command displays failed login attempts and shown in the next example.

Usage syntax: `lastb [OPTIONS] [USER]`

```
$ lastb
nick      tty1                         Sat May 22 13:59 - 13:59  (00:00)
nick      tty1                         Thu May 20 21:27 - 21:27  (00:00)
root      tty1                         Thu May 20 15:27 - 15:27  (00:00)

btmp begins Sat May 20 13:59:28 2010
```

Output of the lastb command

Note	User login/logout activity is stored in the `/var/log/wtmp` file. Failed login attempts are logged in `/var/log/btmp`.

Common usage examples:

`last`	Display the last user login information
`last -[NUMBER]`	Display the specified number of logins
`last [USER]`	Display the last logins for the specified user
`lastb`	Display failed login attempts
`lastb -[NUMBER]`	Display the specified number of failed login attempts
`lastb [USER]`	Display failed login attempts for the specified user

lastlog

Purpose: Display the most recent user login information.

Usage syntax: `lastlog [OPTIONS]`

```
$ lastlog | more
Username        Port      From              Latest
root            tty2                        Sat May 30 11:32:33 -0500 2009
dave            tty3                        Sat May 30 10:22:51 -0500 2009
nick            pts/0     10.10.1.251       Sat May 30 11:31:51 -0500 2009
steve                                       **Never logged in**
bin                                         **Never logged in**
sync                                        **Never logged in**
lp                                          **Never logged in**
...
```

Output of the lastlog command

The `lastlog` command displays the most recent user login time and dates for every user on the system. Executing `lastlog` with no options displays the last login information for all users, as shown in the above example. This output is similar to the `last` command except `lastlog` only displays the most current login activity where `last` displays all available login events.

The `-u` option can be used to display the last login for a specific user as demonstrated in the next example.

```
$ lastlog -u nick
Username        Port      From              Latest
nick            pts/0     10.10.1.251       Sat May 30 11:31:51 -0500 2009
```

Displaying the last login for a specific user

Common usage examples:

`lastlog`	Display the last login information for all users
`lastlog -u [USER]`	Display the last login information for the specified user

finger

Purpose: Display information about a user account.

Usage syntax: `finger [OPTIONS] [USER]`

```
$ finger nick
Login: nick                          Name: Nick Marsh
Directory: /home/nick                Shell: /bin/bash
On since Sat May 30 11:32 (CDT) on tty2   10 minutes 32 seconds idle
New mail received Mon May 17 16:08 2010 (CDT)
    Unread since Tue Apr 13 08:43 2010 (CDT)
No Plan.
```

Using the finger command to display information about a user account

The `finger` command displays information about user accounts. It shows details about the user's shell, home directory, and other helpful information. The example above demonstrates the typical user information displayed when using the `finger` command.

> **Tip**
>
> The `finger` command looks for a file called `.plan` in the specified user's home directory. This file can be edited by the user to contain a note about their status and is displayed whenever they are queried with the `finger` command. If this file does not exist, the `finger` command will display "No Plan" for the user.

Common usage examples:

finger [USER] | Display information about the specified user

passwd

Purpose: Change passwords.

Usage syntax: `passwd [OPTIONS] [USER]`

```
$ passwd
Enter new UNIX password: ******
Retype new UNIX password: ******
passwd: password updated successfully
```
Changing the current user's password

The `passwd` command changes a user's password. Executing `passwd` with no arguments changes the password for the current user as shown in the above example.

The root user can change other user's passwords by specifying a username as demonstrated in the next example.

```
# passwd nick
Enter new UNIX password: ******
Retype new UNIX password: ******
passwd: password updated successfully
```
Changing a specific user's password

Common usage examples:

`passwd`	Set the password for the current user
`passwd [USER]`	Set the password for the specified user
`passwd -e [USER]`	Force a user to change their password at the next login
`passwd -l [USER]`	Lock the specified user account
`passwd -u [USER]`	Unlock the specified user account
`passwd -S [USER]`	Display the status of the specified user account

useradd / userdel

Purpose: Create/delete user accounts.

Usage syntax: `useradd [OPTIONS] [USER]`

```
# useradd -m steve
# passwd steve
Enter new UNIX password: ******
Retype new UNIX password: ******
passwd: password updated successfully
```
Adding a user account to the system (and setting their password)

The `useradd` command creates new user accounts. In the above example, executing `useradd -m steve` creates a basic login account for a user. The `-m` option is used to automatically create a home directory for the specified user (recommended). The password is then set for the new user using the previously discussed `passwd` command.

> **Note** *You must set the password for the new user using the* `passwd` *command before they can login.*

The `userdel` command deletes user accounts from the system. The next example demonstrates using `userdel` to remove an account. The optional `-r` option is used to have the system automatically delete the specified user's home directory after removing their account.

Usage syntax: `userdel [OPTIONS] [USER]`

```
# userdel -r steve
```
Removing a user account

> **Note** *The* `rmuser` *command may be used on some Unix and BSD systems in place of* `userdel`.

Common usage examples:

`useradd [USER]`	Create the specified user account
`useradd -m [USER]`	Automatically create a home directory for the user
`userdel [USER]`	Delete the specified user account
`userdel -r [USER]`	Delete a user's account and their home directory

adduser / deluser

Purpose: Create/delete user accounts on Linux systems.

Usage syntax: adduser [OPTIONS] [USER]

```
# adduser mike
Adding user 'mike' ...
Adding new group 'mike' (1002) ...
Adding new user 'mike' (1002) with group 'mike' ...
Creating home directory '/home/mike' ...
Copying files from '/etc/skel' ...
Enter new UNIX password: ******
Retype new UNIX password: ******
passwd: password updated successfully
Changing the user information for mike
Enter the new value, or press ENTER for the default
        Full Name []: Mike Smith
        Room Number []: Computer Room
        Work Phone []: 555-1212
        Home Phone []:
Is the information correct? [y/N] y
```

Creating a user with the adduser command

The **adduser** command is a user-friendly frontend for the previously discussed **useradd** command. It simplifies the creation of user accounts on Linux systems by prompting for necessary information when creating accounts (rather than having to specify a number of command line options). The above example demonstrates the typical usage of the **adduser** command.

The **deluser** command deletes user accounts as shown in the next example.

Usage syntax: deluser [OPTIONS] [USER]

```
# deluser mike
Removing user 'mike' ...
Warning: Removing group 'mike', since no other user is part of it.
Done.
```

Removing a user with the deluser command

> **Note**
> *Default settings for the* **adduser** *and* **deluser** *commands are stored in* /etc/adduser.conf *and* /etc/deluser.conf.

Common usage examples:

adduser [USER]	Create a user account
deluser [USER]	Remove a user account

groupadd / groupdel

Purpose: Add/remove a group.

Usage syntax: groupadd [GROUP]

```
# groupadd accounting
```

Creating a new group with groupadd

The **groupadd** command creates new group accounts. Groups are helpful in managing access to files and directories in a multiuser environment. In the above example a new group called *accounting* is created. The resulting group entry in the /etc/group file is displayed below.

```
# grep accounting /etc/group
accounting:x:1002:
```

Displaying a group entry in the /etc/group file

The **groupdel** command deletes groups from the system. The next example demonstrates using the **groupdel** command to remove the previously created accounting group from the system

Usage syntax: groupdel [GROUP]

```
# groupdel accounting
```

Deleting a group using groupdel

Common usage examples:

groupadd [GROUP]	Create a new group
groupdel [GROUP]	Delete a group

usermod / groupmod

Purpose: Modify user and group account settings.

Usage syntax: usermod [OPTIONS] [USER]

```
# usermod -aG sales nick
```
Changing a user's group membership using the usermod command

The **usermod** command modifies user account settings. In the above example, the **-aG** option is used to add the user *nick* to the *sales* group. You can also use the **usermod** command to change a user's home directory location using the **-d** option or default shell using **-s**.

The **groupmod** command modifies groups. Its primary purpose is to rename a group. In the next example the *accounting* group is renamed to *finance* using **groupmod -n**.

Usage syntax: groupmod [OPTIONS] [GROUP]

```
# groupmod accounting -n finance
# grep finance /etc/group
finance:x:1002:
```
Renaming a group using the groupmod command

Common usage examples:

usermod -s [SHELL] [USER]	Change a user's default shell
usermod -d [DIR] [USER]	Change a user's home directory location
usermod -aG [GROUP] [USER]	Add a user to the specified group
groupmod [OLD] -n [NEW]	Rename the specified group

wall

Purpose: Broadcast a message to all users on the system.

Usage syntax: `wall [FILE]`

```
# wall
Anyone want some tacos?

<CTRL + D>
```
Using the wall command to send a message to all users logged into the system

The `wall` command sends a message to all users currently logged into the system. The text entered in the above example will display on all local terminals and remote sessions currently logged into the system.

> **Note** Pressing **CTRL + D** *ends the message editor and sends the message.*

The next example displays a sample of the `wall` message output as seen by other users on the system.

```
$

Broadcast Message from root@e6400 (/dev/pts/0) at 11:56 ...

Anyone want some tacos?
```
Output of the wall message displayed on all terminals

In place of manually entering a message, a text file with a prewritten message can be used with the wall command, as shown in the next example.

```
# wall /home/nick/message.txt
```
Using a text file to send a message with the wall command

Common usage examples:

`wall`	Send a message to all users
`wall [FILE]`	Send the message in the specified file to all users

ulimit

Purpose: Display/set system resource limits.

Usage syntax: ulimit [OPTIONS] [LIMIT]

```
$ ulimit -a
core file size          (blocks, -c) 0
data seg size           (kbytes, -d) unlimited
scheduling priority             (-e) 20
file size               (blocks, -f) unlimited
pending signals                 (-i) 16382
max locked memory       (kbytes, -l) 64
max memory size         (kbytes, -m) unlimited
open files                      (-n) 1024
pipe size            (512 bytes, -p) 8
POSIX message queues      (bytes, -q) 819200
real-time priority              (-r) 0
stack size              (kbytes, -s) 8192
cpu time               (seconds, -t) unlimited
max user processes              (-u) unlimited
virtual memory          (kbytes, -v) unlimited
file locks                      (-x) unlimited
```

Displaying defined resource limits using the ulimit command

The ulimit command displays and sets system resource limits. These limits control the maximum amount of system resources available to programs. It can be used to control the maximum amount of memory, CPU time, and file sizes available to each program launched by a user.

> **Tip**
> Ulimit configuration is typically stored in /etc/limits.conf or /etc/security/limits.conf on most systems.

Common usage examples:

ulimit -a	Display all defined resource limits
ulimit [OPTION] [LIMIT]	Set ulimit values

Section 6:
Process Control and Scheduling

Overview

Every program that runs on Unix, Linux, and BSD systems is considered to be a process. Processes are assigned a unique identifier which it used to monitor and control the process. This process identifier (PID) can be used to control processes using the command line utilities discussed in this section.

Commands covered in this section:

Command	Purpose
ps	Display running processes.
pgrep	Find processes by name.
pstree	Display all running processes in a tree view.
kill	Terminate a process.
killall	Terminate all processes with the specified name.
nice	Execute programs at the specified CPU priority level.
renice	Alter the priority of a running process.
&	Start a process in the background.
bg fg	Move a process to the background/foreground.
jobs	Display background and suspended jobs.
nohup	Run a process immune to hang-up signals.
batch	Schedule programs to run during low CPU load.
at	Schedule programs to run at the specified time.
atq	Display queued at jobs.
atrm	Remove scheduled at jobs from the queue.
crontab	Schedule programs to run at the specified time(s).

Glossary of terms used in this section:

Cron	A scheduling system used to execute programs at specific time intervals.
Job	A program that has been scheduled, suspended, or is currently running using the `at` or `batch` scheduling programs.
Nice Value	A numerical indicator assigned to processes to indicate and control their CPU scheduling priority.
PID	(**P**rocess **ID**entifier) A unique numeric value assigned to each process executed on a system.
PPID	(**P**arent **P**rocess **ID**entifier) The PID of the parent process that started a child process.
Priority	Synonym for *Nice Value*.
Process	Any program that has been executed.

ps

Purpose: Display running processes.

Usage syntax: `ps [OPTIONS]`

```
$ ps
  PID TTY          TIME CMD
 4958 pts/0    00:00:00 bash
 9596 pts/0    00:00:00 ps
```
Example output of the ps command

The **ps** command displays running process on the system. Executing the **ps** command with no options will display all processes owned by the current user as shown in the above example. For a complete listing of processes, use the **-e** option as demonstrated in the next example.

```
$ ps -e
  PID TTY          TIME CMD
    1 ?        00:00:01 init
    2 ?        00:00:00 kthreadd
    3 ?        00:00:00 migration/0
    4 ?        00:00:00 ksoftirqd/0
    5 ?        00:00:00 watchdog/0
...
```
Using the -e option with the ps command

The **-ef** option can be used to display detailed information about all processes on the system. This includes the user ID, process ID, parent process ID, and other helpful information, as shown in the next example.

```
$ ps -ef
UID          PID  PPID  C STIME TTY          TIME CMD
root           1     0  0 Jun24 ?        00:00:02 /sbin/init
root           2     0  0 Jun24 ?        00:00:00 [kthreadd]
root           3     2  0 Jun24 ?        00:00:00 [migration/0]
root           4     2  0 Jun24 ?        00:00:00 [ksoftirqd/0]
root           5     2  0 Jun24 ?        00:00:00 [watchdog/0]
...
```
Output of the ps -ef command

Common usage examples:

ps	Display the current user's processes
ps -e	Display all processes running on the system
ps -ef	Display detailed information about running processes
ps -u [USER]	Display processes owned by the specified user

pgrep

Purpose: Find processes by name.

Usage syntax: `pgrep [OPTIONS] [NAME]`

```
$ pgrep apache
3952
4075
4076
4077
4078
4079
```

Displaying PIDs with the name of apache using the pgrep command

The **pgrep** command displays all processes matching the specified name. In the above example the PIDs for the *apache* web server are displayed. This is the equivalent of typing **ps -e|grep apache** and is provided as a shortcut to produce the same results.

The **-l** option can be used with **pgrep** to display the full process name for each PID as demonstrated in the next example.

```
$ pgrep -l apache
3952 apache2
4075 apache2
4076 apache2
4077 apache2
4078 apache2
4079 apache2
```

Using the -l option with pgrep to display the full name of each process

Note	Some systems may use the `pidof` command in place of the `pgrep` command.

Common usage examples:

`pgrep [NAME]`	Display PIDs matching the specified name
`pgrep -l [NAME]`	Display the process name in addition to the PID
`pgrep -P [PPID]`	Display all child processes of the specified PPID
`pgrep -c [NAME]`	Display the total number of matching processes

pstree

Purpose: Display all running processes in a tree view.

Usage syntax: `pstree [OPTIONS]`

```
$ pstree
init──┬─NetworkManager──┬─dhclient
      │                 └─{NetworkManager}
      ├─acpid
      ├─apache2────5*[apache2]
      ├─atd
      ├─cron
      ├─cupsd
      ├─dbus-launch
      ├─dd
      ├─fast-user-switc
      ├─gconfd-2
      ├─6*[getty]
      ├─gnome-keyring-d
      ├─gnome-power-man────{gnome-power-man}
      ├─gnome-screensav
      ├─gnome-settings-────{gnome-settings-}
      ├─gnome-terminal──┬─bash────pstree
      │                 ├─gnome-pty-helpe
      │                 └─{gnome-terminal}
      │
      ├─gvfsd
      ├─gvfsd-burn
...
```

Displaying a process tree using the pstree command

The **pstree** command draws a process tree for all processes currently running on the system, as shown in the above example. The output of **pstree** makes it easy to see the relationship between parent and child processes.

Common usage examples:

`pstree`	Display a basic process tree listing
`pstree -p`	Include PID numbers in the tree listing
`pstree -a`	Include command line options for each process
`pstree [USER]`	Display processes owned by the specified user
`pstree [PID]`	Display child processes of the specified PID

kill

Purpose: Terminate a process.

Usage syntax: `kill [OPTIONS] [PID]`

```
# pgrep -l mysqld
5540 mysqld
# kill 5540
```
Using the kill command to terminate a process

The `kill` command terminates the specified PID. In the above example, the *mysqld* process with a PID of 5540 is terminated using `kill`.

The default behavior of the `kill` command requests the process to gracefully exit. If a process fails to properly terminate, optional kill signals can be sent to force the process to end. The most commonly used kill signal in this situation is `-9` which forcefully terminates the specified PID as displayed in the next example.

```
# pgrep -l mysqld
5545 mysqld
# kill -9 5545
```
Using the -9 option to kill a hung process

Note	It is recommended to only use the `kill -9` command in rare situations where a hung process refuses to gracefully exit. The `-9` signal is only used in these extreme situations, as it can cause undesired results such as system instability and "zombie" child processes.

Common usage examples:

`kill [PID]`	Terminate the specified process
`kill -9 [PID]`	Force an unresponsive process to terminate

killall

Purpose: Terminate all processes with the specified name.

Usage syntax: `killall [OPTIONS] [NAME]`

```
# pgrep -l apache2
3952 apache2
4075 apache2
4076 apache2
4077 apache2
4078 apache2
4079 apache2
# killall apache2
```

Terminating processes by name using the killall command

The `killall` command terminates all processes that match the specified name. This can be helpful if you have several processes with the same name that you need to kill. In the above example, multiple processes related to the *apache2* service are terminated using `killall`.

Tip	The `-i` parameter can be used with `killall` to prompt for confirmation before terminating each process. This is recommended as it helps prevent killing the wrong process due to typos.

Common usage examples:

`killall [NAME]`	Terminate all processes with the specified name
`killall -i [NAME]`	Prompt for confirmation before killing processes

nice

Purpose: Execute programs at the specified CPU priority level.

Usage syntax: `nice [OPTIONS] [COMMAND]`

```
# nice -n 19 LowPriority.sh
# nice -n -20 HighPriority.sh
```
Changing the priority of a process using the nice command

The `nice` command allows programs to be started at a lower or higher than normal scheduling priority. This allows you to control which processes the kernel should favor when dividing processor time among running programs. Processes with the lowest `nice` number are executed with the highest priority and vice versa. The example above demonstrates using `nice` to start programs with modified scheduling priority.

On most systems, priority levels for *normal users* range from 0 to 19, with 0 being the highest priority and 19 being the lowest priority. The *root* user can create processes with a range of -20 (highest) to 19 (lowest).

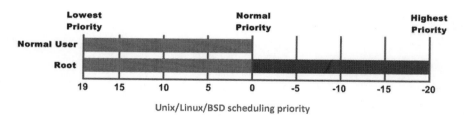

Unix/Linux/BSD scheduling priority

Most programs start with a nice level of 0 by default. Critical system services usually have a negative nice level so that they are always given preference over user programs.

> **Note** *Some Unix systems may use a range of 0 to 39 with 0 being the highest priority and 39 being the lowest. For more information see* `man nice` *on your local system.*

Common usage examples:

`nice -n [NUM] [COMMAND]` | Start a program with the specified priority

renice

Purpose: Alter the priority of a running process.

Usage syntax: `renice [OPTIONS] [PID]`

```
# renice +5 -p 7279
7279: old priority 0, new priority 5
```

Changing the priority of a process

The `renice` command adjusts the priority of a running process. In the above example PID 7279 is adjusted to have a +5 priority. This effectively lowers the priority of the process since the previous priority was 0.

Common usage examples:

`renice +/-[NUM] -p [PID]` | Change the specified PID's priority

&

Purpose: Start a process in the background.

Usage syntax: [COMMAND] &

```
$ ./SomeProgram.sh &
[1] 10717
$ ps
  PID TTY          TIME CMD
10696 pts/0    00:00:00 bash
10717 pts/0    00:00:03 SomeProgram.sh
10721 pts/0    00:00:00 ps
```
Executing a program in the background with the & command line operator

& is a command line operator that instructs the shell to start the specified program in the background. This allows you to have more than one program running at the same time without having to start multiple terminal sessions. In the above example, a shell script called SomeProgram.sh is started as a background process. Executing the **ps** command shows the requested program is now running in the background.

> **Tip**
> *Output from background programs will still be displayed in the shell. You can redirect this output to a file by using the following syntax:* **SomeProgram.sh > output.log &** *This will redirect all the output of the background program to a file called* output.log *in the current directory.*

Common usage examples:

[COMMAND] &	Execute the specified command in the background
[COMMAND] > [FILE] &	Redirect the output of the background command to a file

bg / fg

Purpose: Move a process to the background/foreground.

Usage syntax: `bg [JOBID]`

```
$ ./SomeProgram.sh
<CTRL + Z>
[1]+  Stopped                 SomeProgram.sh
$ bg 1
$ jobs
[1]-  Running                 SomeProgram.sh
```

Suspending a running program and then resuming it in the background

The `bg` command sends a process to the background. This allows you to multitask several programs within a single terminal session. In the above example the shell script `SomeProgram.sh` is suspended (by pressing **CTRL + Z** on the keyboard) and then resumed as a background process using `bg`.

> **Note**
> The `jobs` command (see page 126) can be used to verify the program is now running in the background.

The `fg` command moves background processes to the foreground. In the next example the `fg` command is used to bring the specified job ID to the foreground.

Usage syntax: `fg [JOBID]`

```
$ jobs
[1]-  Running                 SomeProgram.sh
$ fg 1
SomeProgram.sh
...
```

Moving a background job to the foreground

Common usage examples:

`bg [JOBID]`	Send the specified job to the background
`fg [JOBID]`	Move the specified job to the foreground

jobs

Purpose: Display background and suspended jobs.

Usage syntax: `jobs [OPTIONS]`

```
$ jobs
[1]-  Running                 SomeProgram.sh
[2]+  Stopped                 AnotherProgram.sh
[3]   Stopped                 Test.sh
```
Displaying background programs using the jobs command

The `jobs` command displays the status of background programs and suspended processes. In the above example, three background jobs are displayed. The previously mentioned `fg` and `bg` commands can be used to move the processes to the foreground and background respectively.

The following table describes the output fields of the `jobs` command.

Job ID	Status	Program
[1]-	Running	SomeProgram.sh
[2]+	Stopped	AnotherProgram.sh
[3]	Stopped	Test.sh

Output fields of the jobs command

Note	*The plus sign is used to indicate what job is considered to be the default job (for use with the `bg` and `fg` commands). The minus sign indicates the job that will become the default if the current default job terminates. There can be only one + and - at any given time. All other jobs will not have any indicators.*

Common usage examples:

jobs	Display all jobs
jobs -l	Display all jobs and their PID

nohup

Purpose: Run a process immune to hang-up signals.

Usage syntax: `nohup [COMMAND] &`

```
$ nohup SomeProgram.sh &
nohup: ignoring input and appending output to 'nohup.out'
$ exit
```
Using the nohup command to launch a background program

The `nohup` command makes processes immune to hang-up signals. A hang-up signal is used to inform child processes of a shell that the parent process is terminating. This would normally cause all child processes to terminate. Using `nohup` allows a program to continue running after you log out, as demonstrated in the above example.

> **Tip** *Output from the program is stored in a file called* `nohup.out` *in the directory where the nohup command was executed.*

Common usage examples:

`nohup [COMMAND ] &` | Execute a program immune to hang-up signals

at / atq / atrm

Purpose: Schedule a program to run at the specified time.

Usage syntax: `at [OPTIONS] [TIME|DATE]`

```
$ at 1am
at> MyProgram.sh
at> <CTRL + D>
job 1 at Sat May 30 01:00:00 2009
```
Scheduling a process using the at command

The `at` command schedules programs to run at the specified time. In the above example, the `at` command is used to launch a shell script called **MyProgram.sh**. The launch time in this example is specified as `1am` on the command line. You can also use more traditional Unix time specifications such as 01:00 or any other HH:MM combination.

Tip	*The `at` command has a special command line argument called `now`. This can be used as a shortcut to save time when scheduling jobs. For example typing `at now + 15 minutes` would schedule the job to launch 15 minutes from the current time.*

The `atq` command displays information about queued `at` jobs as shown in the next example.

Usage syntax: `atq`

```
$ atq
1        Sat May 30 01:00:00 2009 MyProgram.sh nick
```
Using the atq command to display the job queue

The `atrm` command deletes a scheduled job as shown in the next example.

Usage syntax: `atrm [JOBID]`

```
$ atrm 1
```
Removing a scheduled job using the atrm command

Common usage examples:

`at [TIME]`	Schedule a program to run at the specified time
`atq`	Display the `at` job queue
`atrm [JOBID]`	Remove a scheduled job from the `at` queue

batch

Purpose: Schedule programs to run during low CPU load.

Usage syntax: `batch [OPTIONS]`

```
$ batch
at> BigProgram.sh
at> <CTRL + D>
job 1 at Fri May 29 20:01:00 200
```
Scheduling a batch process

The `batch` command schedules a program to run when the system CPU load is low. This is useful for running resource-intensive programs that would normally interfere with system performance.

In this example the `batch` program is used to schedule the `BigProgram.sh` script to run when the system CPU load is low.

> **Note**
> *Each platform has its own definition of low load. See* **man batch** *for more information about your system's* **batch** *command usage.*

Common usage examples:

`batch` | Launch the batch scheduling shell

crontab

Purpose: Schedule programs to run at the specified time(s).

Usage syntax: `crontab [OPTIONS]`

```
# crontab -l
30 12 * * 1-5 /root/SomeProgram.sh
```
Displaying configured cron jobs

The `crontab` command manages a user's scheduled cron jobs. Cron is a subsystem found on most Unix, Linux, and BSD systems that schedules programs to run at a specific interval. It differs from the previously discussed `at` command because cron jobs run at reoccurring intervals (where `at` jobs run only once).

Note	*The name cron comes from the Greek word "chronos" which means "time".*

In the above example, the `-l` option is used to display the current user's crontab. The table below describes the fields found in the crontab file.

Minute	Hour	Day of Month	Month	Day of Week	Program
30	12	*	*	1-5	/root/SomeProgram.sh

Crontab fields

In this example `SomeProgram.sh` is run every Monday-Friday at 12:30 PM. The day of week is symbolized as 0=Sunday, 1=Monday, 2=Tuesday, etc. An asterisk (*) is a wild card that represents all valid values.

`crontab -e` is used to edit the current user's crontab as demonstrated in the next example.

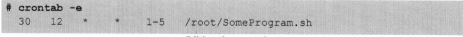
```
# crontab -e
  30   12   *    *    1-5   /root/SomeProgram.sh
```
Editing the crontab

Common usage examples:

`crontab -l`	List the current user's crontab
`crontab -e`	Edit the current user's crontab
`crontab -r`	Delete the current user's crontab

130

Section 7: Startup and Shutdown

Overview

This chapter covers commands used to startup and shutdown Unix, Linux, and BSD systems. It also provides an overview of platform specific service control commands for popular platforms.

Commands covered in this section:

Command	Purpose
shutdown	Shut down the system.
poweroff	Power off the system.
reboot	Reboot the system.
halt	Halt the system.
telinit	Change the runlevel.
runlevel	Display the previous and current runlevel.
service	Manage services on a Linux system.
sysv-rc-conf	Display and edit Linux runlevel configuration.
chkconfig	Display and edit runlevel configuration on Red Hat Linux-based systems.
rc-update	Display and edit runlevel configuration on Gentoo Linux systems.
rc-status	Display the status of services on Gentoo Linux systems.
stopsrc startsrc	Stop/start services on AIX systems.
lssrc	Display the status of services on AIX systems.
svcs	Display the status of services on Solaris systems.
svcadm	Start/stop services on Solaris systems.

Glossary of terms used in this section:

Init	(**INIT**ialization) A program that controls the startup (AKA initialization) of Unix, Linux, and BSD systems.
Runlevel	A set of profiles used by the init program that defines the programs and services to load during system startup (or when called by the `telinit` command).
Service	A system program that provides a service as a web server, DNS server, email server, etc. Services are sometimes referred to as *Daemons* or *Service Daemons*.

shutdown

Purpose: Shut down the system.

Usage syntax: `shutdown [OPTIONS] [TIME] [MESSAGE]`

```
# shutdown now
BROADCAST MESSAGE FROM ROOT:
The system is going down for shutdown now!
* Stopping services                                          [ OK ]
* Terminating processes                                      [ OK ]
...
The system will now halt.
```

Example output from the shutdown command

The `shutdown` command is used to shutdown the local system. There are several different types of shutdowns that can be performed: halt, poweroff, and reboot.

> **Note**
>
> *Usage of the* `shutdown` *command varies between the various Unix, Linux, and BSD platforms. Examples on this page are intended for Linux systems. For usage examples specific to your environment, type* **man** **shutdown** *on your local system.*

When the `shutdown` command is executed, a warning is broadcast to all users logged in to the local system. An optional message can be specified following the time argument as shown in the next example.

```
# shutdown 2 Save your work and log off ASAP!
BROADCAST MESSAGE FROM ROOT:
The system is going down for shutdown in 2 minutes!
Save your work and log off ASAP!
```

Example output from the shutdown command's broadcast message

Common usage examples:

`shutdown now`	Shutdown the system immediately
`shutdown [MIN]`	Wait the specified number of minutes before shutting down
`shutdown [HH:MM]`	Shutdown at the specified time (24-hour format)
`shutdown -r now`	Restart the system
`shutdown -H now`	Halt the system
`shutdown -P now`	Power off the system

poweroff

Purpose: Power off the system.

Usage syntax: `poweroff`

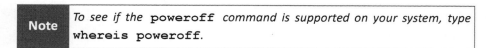

```
# poweroff
BROADCAST MESSAGE FROM ROOT:
The system is going down for power off now!
* Stopping services                                    [ OK ]
* Terminating processes                                [ OK ]
...
The system will now power off.
```

Example output of the poweroff command

The `poweroff` command will immediately shutdown and power off the system. It is essentially a shortcut for `shutdown -P now`. The `poweroff` command is found on all Linux distributions and some BSD and Unix systems.

Note	*To see if the* `poweroff` *command is supported on your system, type* `whereis poweroff`.

Warning	*The* `poweroff` *command does not offer a grace period and will immediately bring down the system when executed.*

Common usage examples:

`poweroff`	Shutdown and poweroff the system

reboot

Purpose: Reboot the system.

Usage syntax: `reboot`

```
# reboot
BROADCAST MESSAGE FROM ROOT: The system is going down for reboot now!

* Stopping services                                              [ OK ]
* Terminating processes                                          [ OK ]
...
The system will now reboot.
```
Example output of the reboot command

The `reboot` command is used to gracefully reboot the system. It is essentially a shortcut for `shutdown -r now`. Executing `reboot` on the command line will immediately reboot the system as demonstrated in the above example.

Warning	*The* `reboot` *command does not offer a grace period and will immediately reboot the system when executed.*

Common usage examples:

`reboot`	Gracefully reboot the system

halt

Purpose: Halt the system.

Usage syntax: `halt`

```
# halt
BROADCAST MESSAGE FROM ROOT: The system is going down for halt now!

* Stopping services                                              [ OK ]
* Terminating processes                                          [ OK ]
...
The system will now halt.
```

Example output of the halt command

The `halt` command will halt an online system. A halt is a special type of shutdown which gracefully shuts down the operating system without powering off the system.

Note	*Some commercial Unix systems will enter maintenance mode when halted. This can be used to access a pre-boot configuration/diagnostic environment.*

Common usage examples:

`halt` | Halt the system

telinit

Purpose: Change the runlevel.

Usage syntax: `telinit [RUNLEVEL]`

```
# telinit 1
*** Switching to run level 1 ***
# runlevel
3 1
```
Using telinit to change the system's runlevel

`telinit` tells the system's *init* process to stop and start the necessary services configured for the specified runlevel. In the above example the `telinit` command is used to change the system to runlevel 1. The `runlevel` command (see page 138) is then executed to display the current and previous runlevels.

Each system's runlevel configuration is specific to the distribution being used and can be customized to fit your needs. Most Unix, Linux, and BSD systems will have a runlevel configuration similar to the one described in the following table.

Runlevel	Purpose
0	Shutdown or special administrative mode
1	Single user mode
2	Multiuser mode
3	Multiuser mode
4	Multiuser mode
5	Distribution specific
6	Reboot

Typical Unix, Linux, and BSD runlevels

Common usage examples:

`telinit [RUNLEVEL]` | Tell the init process to load the specified runlevel

runlevel

Purpose: Display the previous and current runlevel.

Usage syntax: `runlevel`

```
$ runlevel
3 1
```

Output of the runlevel command

The **runlevel** command displays the current and previous runlevel. The runlevel is an initialization sequence called by the *init* process and defines procedures for system startup and shutdown. In the above example, **runlevel** is used to display the current runlevel information. The first number displayed is the previous runlevel and the second number is the current runlevel.

Note	*If there is no previous runlevel, the system will display* N *in the first field.*

Common usage examples:

runlevel | Display the previous and current runlevel

service

Purpose: Manage services on a Linux system.

Usage syntax: `service [OPTIONS] [SERVICE] [ACTION]`

```
# service --status-all
 [ + ]  acpid
 [ - ]  anacron
 [ + ]  apache2
 [ + ]  atd
 [ + ]  cups
 [ + ]  dbus
 [ + ]  gdm
 [ + ]  hal
 [ + ]  klogd
 [ + ]  ssh
 [ + ]  sysklogd
 ...
```

Displaying the status of services with the service command

The **service** command manages services on Linux systems. In the above example, the **--status-all** option displays the status of all services on the system. The **+** symbol indicates a running service and the **−** symbol indicates a stopped service.

The **start**, **stop**, **restart**, and **status** options can be used to control individual services as demonstrated in the next example.

```
# service ssh stop
 * Stopping OpenBSD Secure Shell server sshd                      [ OK ]
# service ssh start
 * Starting OpenBSD Secure Shell server sshd                      [ OK ]
# service ssh restart
 * Restarting OpenBSD Secure Shell server sshd                    [ OK ]
# service ssh status
 * sshd is running
```

Stopping, starting, restarting, and viewing the status of services

Common usage examples:

`service [SERVICE] stop`	Stop the specified service
`service [SERVICE] start`	Start the specified service
`service [SERVICE] restart`	Restart the specified service
`service [SERVICE] status`	Display the status of the specified service
`service --status-all`	Display the status of all services

sysv-rc-conf

Purpose: Display and edit Linux runlevel configuration.

Usage syntax: `sysv-rc-conf [OPTIONS] [SERVICE] [ON|OFF]`

```
# sysv-rc-conf
 ┌ SysV Runlevel Config   -: stop service  =/+: start service  h: help  q: quit ┐
 │ service       1       2       3       4       5       0       6       S       │
 │ ---------------------------------------------------------------------------   │
 │ acpid        [ ]     [X]     [X]     [X]     [X]     [ ]     [ ]     [ ]       │
 │ anacron      [ ]     [X]     [X]     [X]     [X]     [ ]     [ ]     [ ]       │
 │ apache       [ ]     [X]     [X]     [X]     [X]     [ ]     [ ]     [ ]       │
 │ apparmor     [ ]     [ ]     [ ]     [ ]     [ ]     [ ]     [ ]     [X]       │
 │ apport       [ ]     [X]     [X]     [X]     [X]     [ ]     [ ]     [ ]       │
 │ atd          [ ]     [X]     [X]     [X]     [X]     [ ]     [ ]     [ ]       │
 │ bind9        [ ]     [X]     [X]     [X]     [X]     [ ]     [ ]     [ ]       │
 └───────────────────────────────────────────────────────────────────────────── ┘
 ┌─────────────────────────────────────────────────────────────────────────────┐
 │ Use the arrow keys or mouse to move around.      ^n: next pg    ^p: prev pg │
 │                    space: toggle service on / off                           │
 └─────────────────────────────────────────────────────────────────────────────┘
```

Example output of the sysv-rc-conf command

The **sysv-rc-conf** command manages service/runlevel configuration on Linux systems. In the above example, executing **sysv-rc-conf** starts a configuration utility which enables the user to select which services start on the various runlevels.

Services can also be displayed and modified via the command line using the **--list** and **--level** options as demonstrated in the next example.

```
# sysv-rc-conf --level 2345 apache off
# sysv-rc-conf --list apache2
apache2      2:off   3:off   4:off   5:off
# sysv-rc-conf --level 2345 apache2 on
# sysv-rc-conf --list apache2
apache2      2:on    3:on    4:on    5:on
```

Using the sysv-rc-conf command to mange services on the command line

Common usage examples:

`sysv-rc-conf`	Display the runlevel configuration utility
`sysv-rc-conf --list`	List runlevel configuration for all services
`sysv-rc-conf --level \` `[LEVEL] [SERVICE] on`	Enable a service on the specified level(s)
`sysv-rc-conf --level \` `[LEVEL] [SERVICE] off`	Disable a service on the specified level(s)

chkconfig

Purpose: Display and edit runlevel configuration on Red Hat Linux-based systems.

Usage syntax: `chkconfig [OPTIONS] [SERVICE] [ON|OFF] [LEVEL]`

```
# chkconfig -l
acpi-support          0:off  1:off  2:on   3:on   4:on   5:on   6:off
acpid                 0:off  1:off  2:on   3:on   4:on   5:on   6:off
alsa-utils            0:off  1:off  2:off  3:off  4:off  5:off  6:off
anacron               0:off  1:off  2:on   3:on   4:on   5:on   6:off
apache2               0:off  1:off  2:off  3:off  4:off  5:off  6:off
apport                0:off  1:off  2:on   3:on   4:on   5:on   6:off
...
```

Listing service configuration with the chkconfig command

The `chkconfig` command manages services on Red Hat Linux systems. The `-l` parameter lists the current runlevel configuration, as shown in the above example. If no service is specified, all services will be displayed. Specifying a service name will display the runlevel configuration for the service, as shown in the next example.

```
# chkconfig -l apache2
apache2               0:off  1:off  2:on   3:on   4:on   5:on   6:off
```

Listing a specific service with the chkconfig command

The `-s` option is used to enable or disable services at the specified run levels as demonstrated in the next example.

```
# chkconfig -s apache2 off 2345
# chkconfig -l apache2
apache2               0:off  1:off  2: off 3: off 4: off 5:off 6:off
# chkconfig -s apache2 on 2345
# chkconfig -l apache2
apache2               0:off  1:off  2:on   3:on   4:on   5:on   6:off
```

Managing services with the chkconfig command

Common usage examples:

`chkconfig -l`	List runlevel configuration for all services
`chkconfig -l [SERVICE]`	List a service's current configuration
`chkconfig -s [SERVICE] \` `on [LEVEL]`	Enable a service on the specified level(s)
`chkconfig -s [SERVICE] \` `off [LEVEL]`	Disable a service on the specified level(s)

rc-status

Purpose: Display the status of services on Gentoo Linux systems.

Usage syntax: `rc-status [OPTIONS]`

```
# rc-status
Runlevel: default
 amavisd                                            [ started ]
 apache2                                            [ started ]
 clamd                                              [ started ]
 courier-authlib                                    [ started ]
 courier-imapd                                      [ started ]
 courier-imapd-ssl                                  [ started ]
 courier-pop3d                                      [ started ]
 hostname                                           [ started ]
 keymaps                                            [ started ]
 ...
```

Output of the rc-status command

The **rc-status** displays the status of services on Gentoo Linux systems. In the above example, all services for the current level are listed along with their current status.

Note	Gentoo Linux uses a nontraditional init structure that differs from most Linux systems. You can read more about Gentoo's init system online at www.gentoo.org/doc/en/handbook/.

Common usage examples:

rc-status	List services for the current runlevel
rc-status -a	List all services
rc-status -l	List all defined run levels

rc-update

Purpose: Display and edit runlevel configuration on Gentoo Linux systems.

Usage syntax: `rc-update [OPTIONS] [SERVICE] [LEVEL]`

```
# rc-update show
             amavisd |        default
             apache2 |        default
            bootmisc | boot
              checkfs | boot
           checkroot | boot
               clamd |        default
               clock | boot
          consolefont | boot
      courier-authlib |        default
       courier-imapd |        default
   courier-imapd-ssl |        default
       courier-pop3d |        default
   courier-pop3d-ssl |        default
   ...
```

Using the rc-update command to display runlevel configuration

The `rc-update` command manages services on Gentoo Linux-based systems. In the above example, the **show** option is used to display the current runlevel configuration.

The **add** and **del** options are used to add and delete services from the specified runlevel, as shown in the next example.

```
# rc-update add sshd default
 * sshd added to runlevel default
# rc-update del sshd default
 * 'sshd' removed from the following runlevels: default
```

Adding and removing services to the default runlevel using rc-update

Common usage examples:

`rc-update show`	List runlevel configuration for all services
`rc-update add \` `[SERVICE] default`	Add the specified service to the default runlevels
`rc-update del \` `[SERVICE] default`	Remove the specified service from the default runlevels

lssrc

Purpose: Display the status of services on AIX systems.

Usage syntax: `lssrc [OPTIONS] [SERVICE/GROUP]`

```
# lssrc -a
Subsystem            Group          PID        Status
 syslogd             ras            147590     active
 sendmail            mail           188508     active
 portmap             portmap        126980     active
 snmpmibd            tcpip          151728     active
 inetd               tcpip          163958     active
 snmpd               tcpip          180316     active
 hostmibd            tcpip          159852     active
 aixmibd             tcpip          168024     active
 biod                nfs            196706     active
 rpc.statd           nfs            209038     active
 rpc.lockd           nfs            204984     active
 qdaemon             spooler        217200     active
 writesrv            spooler        233588     active
 ctrmc               rsct           241870     active
 pconsole            pconsole       270470     active
 cimsys                             229504     active
 IBM.ServiceRM       rsct_rm        311470     active
 IBM.CSMAgentRM      rsct_rm        291004     active
 lpd                 spooler                   inoperative
...
```
Listing the status of all services

The `lssrc` command displays the status of services on AIX systems. The above example demonstrates using the `-a` option to display the status of all services. The next example demonstrates using the `-s` option to list a specific service.

```
# lssrc -s nfsd
Subsystem            Group          PID        Status
 nfsd                nfs                       inoperative
```
Listing a specific service

Common usage examples:

`lssrc -a`	Display the status of all services
`lssrc -s [SERVICE]`	Display the status of the specified services
`lssrc -g [GROUP]`	Display the status of the specified group of services

stopsrc / startsrc

Purpose: Start/stop services on AIX systems.

Usage syntax: `startsrc [OPTIONS] [SERVICE/GROUP]`

```
# startsrc -s nfsd
0513-059 The nfsd Subsystem has been started. Subsystem PID is 221400.
```
Starting a service on AIX with startsrc

The `startsrc` command starts services (known as SRCs or system resource controllers) on AIX systems. The above example demonstrates using the `startsrc` command to start the NFS service.

The `stopsrc` command stops services on AIX systems. The next example demonstrates using `stopsrc` to stop the NFS service.

Usage syntax: `startsrc [OPTIONS] [SERVICE/GROUP]`

```
# stopsrc -s nfsd
0513-044 The nfsd Subsystem was requested to stop.
```
Stopping a service on AIX with stopsrc

Common usage examples:

`startsrc -s [SERVICE]`	Start the specified service
`stopsrc -s [SERVICE]`	Stop the specified service
`startsrc -g [GROUP]`	Start the specified group of services
`stopsrc -g [GROUP]`	Stop the specified group of services
`stopsrc -a`	Stop all running services

svcs

Purpose: Display the status of services on Solaris systems.

Usage syntax: `svcs [OPTIONS] [SERVICE]`

```
# svcs
STATE              STIME     FMRI
legacy_run         19:41:19  lrc:/etc/rcS_d/S50sk98sol
legacy_run         19:42:11  lrc:/etc/rc2_d/S101u
legacy_run         19:42:11  lrc:/etc/rc2_d/S20sysetup
legacy_run         19:42:11  lrc:/etc/rc2_d/S4011c2
legacy_run         19:42:12  lrc:/etc/rc2_d/S42ncakmod
legacy_run         19:42:13  lrc:/etc/rc2_d/S47pppd
legacy_run         19:42:13  lrc:/etc/rc2_d/S70uucp
legacy_run         19:42:13  lrc:/etc/rc2_d/S72autoinstall
legacy_run         19:42:13  lrc:/etc/rc2_d/S73cachefs_daemon
legacy_run         19:42:14  lrc:/etc/rc2_d/S81dodatadm_udaplt
legacy_run         19:42:14  lrc:/etc/rc2_d/S89PRESERVE
legacy_run         19:42:14  lrc:/etc/rc2_d/S94ncalogd
legacy_run         19:42:15  lrc:/etc/rc2_d/S98deallocate
legacy_run         19:42:16  lrc:/etc/rc3_d/S16boot_server
legacy_run         19:42:17  lrc:/etc/rc3_d/S50apache
...
```
Listing services on a Solaris system with the svcs command

The **svcs** command displays the status of services on Solaris systems. Executing **svcs** with no options will list all active services, as shown in the example above.

To see the status of an individual service, a service name can be specified as demonstrated in the next example.

```
# svcs apache
STATE              STIME     FMRI
legacy_run         19:42:17  lrc:/etc/rc3_d/S50apache
```
Listing the status of an individual service using the svcs command

Common usage examples:

`svcs`	Display all active services
`svcs -a`	Display all services
`svcs [SERVICE]`	Display the specified service
`svcs -d [SERVICE]`	Display the specified service's dependencies
`svcs -D [SERVICE]`	Display services that depend on the specified service
`svcs -l [SERVICE]`	Display detailed information about the specified service

svcadm

Purpose: Start/stop services on Solaris systems.

Usage syntax: `svcadm [OPTIONS] [SERVICE]`

```
# svcadm enable sendmail
# svcs sendmail
STATE          STIME    FMRI
online         14:26:14 svc:/network/smtp:sendmail
```
Starting a service with the svcadm command

The `svcadm` command controls services on Solaris systems. It can be used to start, stop, and restart services. In the above example, the `enable` parameter is used to start the sendmail service. The next example demonstrates using the `disable` parameter to stop the sendmail service.

```
# svcadm disable sendmail
# svcs sendmail
STATE          STIME    FMRI
disabled       14:27:51 svc:/network/smtp:sendmail
```
Stopping a service with the svcadm command

To restart a service, use the `restart` parameter as demonstrated in the next example.

```
# svcadm restart sendmail
```
Restarting a service with the svcadm command

Common usage examples:

`svcadm enable [SERVICE]`	Start the specified service
`svcadm disable [SERVICE]`	Stop the specified service
`svcadm restart [SERVICE]`	Restart the specified service

Section 8: Network Commands

Overview

This section covers basic networking utilities and configuration commands found on most platforms. It also provides an overview of remote access to network-based services like SSH, NFS, and FTP.

Commands covered in this section:

Command	Purpose
hostname	Display the system's host name.
ifconfig	Display network interfaces.
ifup ifdown	Enable/disable network interfaces.
iwconfig	Display wireless network interfaces.
ethtool	Display and edit ethernet card settings.
arp	Display the ARP cache.
ping	Send ICMP echo requests to network hosts.
traceroute	Display TCP/IP routing information.
tracepath	Display TCP/IP routing information on Linux systems.
nslookup	Perform DNS lookups on Unix systems.
dig	Perform DNS lookups on BSD and Linux systems.
host	Simple DNS lookup utility.
whois	Lookup domain name registry information in the whois database.
netstat	Display network connections, statistics, and routing information.
route	Display and configure TCP/IP routes.
ifstat	Display network interface statistics.
tcpdump	Display raw traffic on a network interface.
dhclient	DHCP client for Linux and BSD systems.
nmap	Scan TCP/IP ports on network systems.
telnet	Client for connecting to remote servers via the telnet protocol.
ssh	Client for connecting to remote servers via the SSH protocol.

(Continued...)

Command	Purpose
minicom	Serial communication application.
mail	Send email to local and remote users.
ftp	Transfer files using FTP (File Transfer Protocol).
wget	File download utility for Linux systems.
showmount	Display NFS mount and export information.

Glossary of terms used in this section:

ARP	(**A**ddress **R**esolution **P**rotocol) Protocol for resolving MAC addresses.
DHCP	(**D**ynamic **H**ost **C**onfiguration **P**rotocol) Protocol for automatically assigning IP addresses.
DNS	(**D**omain **N**ame **S**ystem) System that resolves host names to IP addresses.
FTP	(**F**ile **T**ransfer **P**rotocol) Protocol used to transfer files to and from remote systems.
Hostname	The name assigned to a computer system.
ICMP	(**I**nternet **C**ontrol **M**essage **P**rotocol) Protocol used to relay error messages to network systems.
Loopback	A virtual network interface found on Unix, Linux, and BSD systems used to communicate with network services on the local machine.
MAC Address	(**M**edia **A**ccess **C**ontrol Address) A unique identifier assigned to network interfaces.
NFS	(**N**etwork **F**ile **S**ystem) Protocol used to share storage via a network on Unix, Linux, and BSD systems.
Packet	A unit of data transmitted between network systems.
Route	The path a packet travels across a network to the destination.
Serial	A legacy form of communication used to link devices together.
Telnet	A legacy protocol for connecting to remote systems.
SSH	(**S**ecure **SH**ell) A secure protocol for connecting to remote systems.

hostname

Purpose: Display the system's host name.

Usage syntax: `hostname [OPTIONS]`

```
# hostname
mylaptop
```
Displaying the system's hostname

The `hostname` command displays the name assigned to the local system. The above example demonstrates the typical output of the `hostname` command.

`hostname` can also be used to display the system's domain name as demonstrated in the next example.

```
# hostname -d
mydomain.com
```
Displaying the system's domain name

Using the `-f` option, you can see the the system's FQDN (**F**ully **Q**ualified **D**omain **N**ame) as show in the below example.

```
# hostname -f
mylaptop.mydomain.com
```
Displaying the system's FQDN

> **Note** *Host name configuration is stored in* `/etc/hostname` *on most systems.*

Common usage examples:

`hostname`	Display the system's host name
`hostname -d`	Display the system's domain name
`hostname -f`	Display the system's fully qualified domain name

ifconfig

Purpose: Display network interfaces.

Usage syntax: ifconfig [OPTIONS] [INTERFACE]

```
$ ifconfig -a
eth0      Link encap:Ethernet  HWaddr 00:21:70:ac:f7:e7
          inet addr:10.10.1.100  Bcast:10.10.1.255  Mask:255.255.255.0
          inet6 addr:  fe80::221:70ff:feac:f7e7/64 Scope:Link
          UP BROADCAST RUNNING MULTICAST  MTU:1500  Metric:1
          RX packets:2937 errors:0 dropped:0 overruns:0 frame:0
          TX packets:2088 errors:0 dropped:0 overruns:0 carrier:0
          collisions:0 txqueuelen:1000
          RX bytes:2199807 (2.1 MB)  TX bytes:548839 (548.8 KB)
          Memory:f6fe0000-f7000000

lo        Link encap:Local Loopback
          inet addr:127.0.0.1  Mask:255.0.0.0
          inet6 addr:  ::1/128 Scope:Host
          UP LOOPBACK RUNNING  MTU:16436  Metric:1
          RX packets:316 errors:0 dropped:0 overruns:0 frame:0
          TX packets:316 errors:0 dropped:0 overruns:0 carrier:0
          collisions:0 txqueuelen:0
          RX bytes:26552 (26.5 KB)  TX bytes:26552 (26.5 KB)
```

Using the ifconfig command to display network interfaces

The `ifconfig` command displays the system's network interface configuration. The output of `ifconfig` displays information such as IP address, MAC address, and interface statistical counters, as shown in the above example.

The most common type of network interface is a standard ethernet card. This interface is usually designated as `eth0` or `en0`. Systems with multiple network cards will have `eth0`, `eth1`, `eth2`, etc.

| Note | *The loopback interface (`lo`) is present on all Unix, Linux, and BSD systems. It is critical for normal system operations and should not be disabled or modified. This interface will always have an IP address of 127.0.0.1.* |

Common usage examples:

`ifconfig`	Display enabled network interfaces
`ifconfig -a`	Display all network interfaces
`ifconfig [INTERFACE]`	Display the specified network interface

ifup / ifdown

Purpose: Enable/disable network interfaces.

Usage syntax: `ifup [OPTIONS] [INTERFACE]`

```
# ifup eth0
```
Enabling a network interface using the ifup command

`ifup` enables a network interface. In the above example the interface `eth0` is enabled. After executing the `ifup` command, the `eth0` interface is activated and available for use.

`ifdown` disables network interfaces. This takes the specified interface offline and makes it unavailable for use. The next example demonstrates using `ifdown` to shutdown the `eth0` interface.

Usage syntax: `ifdown [OPTIONS] [INTERFACE]`

```
# ifdown eth0
```
Disabling a network interface using the ifdown command

> **Note** *Some systems may designate ethernet interfaces as* `en0` *instead of* `eth0`.

Common usage examples:

`ifup [INTERFACE]`	Enable the specified network interface
`ifup -a`	Enable all network interfaces
`ifdown [INTERFACE]`	Disable the specified network interface
`ifdown -a`	Disable all network interfaces

iwconfig

Purpose: Display wireless network interfaces.

Usage syntax: `iwconfig [INTERFACE] [OPTIONS]`

```
$ iwconfig
wlan0  IEEE 802.11abgn  ESSID:"my-wlan"
       Mode:Managed  Frequency:2.437 GHz  Access Point: 00:14:BF:E4:1B:E2
       Bit Rate=54 Mb/s   Tx-Power=15 dBm
       Retry min limit:7   RTS thr:off   Fragment thr=2352 B
       Power Management:off
       Link Quality=97/100  Signal level:-52 dBm  Noise level=-91 dBm
       Rx invalid nwid:0  Rx invalid crypt:0  Rx invalid frag:0
       Tx excessive retries:0  Invalid misc:0   Missed beacon:0
```

Displaying wireless network interfaces using the iwconfig command

`iwconfig` displays wireless network interfaces on Linux systems. It is similar to the previously discussed `ifconfig` command, except it displays information specific to wireless networks.

In the above example the information for the `wlan0` interface is displayed. It shows information such as signal level, noise level, and transmission rate for the connected wireless network.

Common usage examples:

`iwconfig`	Display all wireless network interfaces
`iwconfig [INTERFACE]`	Display the specified wireless network interface

ethtool

Purpose: Display ethernet card settings.

Usage syntax: ethtool [OPTIONS] [INTERFACE]

```
# ethtool eth0
Settings for eth0:
        Supported ports: [ TP ]
        Supported link modes:   10baseT/Half 10baseT/Full
                                100baseT/Half 100baseT/Full
                                1000baseT/Full
        Supports auto-negotiation: Yes
        Advertised link modes:  10baseT/Half 10baseT/Full
                                100baseT/Half 100baseT/Full
                                1000baseT/Full
        Advertised pause frame use: No
        Advertised auto-negotiation: Yes
        Link partner advertised link modes:  Not reported
        Link partner advertised pause frame use: No
        Link partner advertised auto-negotiation: No
        Speed: 100Mb/s
...
```

Typical output of the ethtool command

ethtool is a Linux utility for displaying information about network interfaces. The default output displays advanced network interface settings as displayed in the above example. It can also be used to display network statistics using the -S parameter as shown in the next example.

```
# ethtool -S eth0
NIC statistics:
     rx_packets: 125
     tx_packets: 114
     rx_bytes: 14459
     tx_bytes: 17596
     rx_broadcast: 9
     tx_broadcast: 3
     rx_multicast: 14
     tx_multicast: 19
     rx_errors: 0
...
```

Displaying interface statistics using the -S parameter

Common usage examples:

ethtool [INTERFACE]	Display network interface settings
ethtool -S [INTERFACE]	Display network interface statistics

arp

Purpose: Display the ARP cache.

Usage syntax: `arp [OPTIONS]`

```
$ arp
Address           HWtype   HWaddress            Flags Mask          Iface
10.10.2.1         ether    00:06:B1:12:0D:16    C                   eth1
10.10.2.5         ether    00:14:22:0E:35:5C    C                   eth1
10.10.2.6         ether    00:0C:29:1E:10:70    C                   eth1
10.10.2.7         ether    00:0C:29:C1:02:C0    C                   eth1
10.10.2.10        ether    00:0C:29:38:00:F6    C                   eth1
```

Output of the arp command

The **arp** command displays the ARP cache. Local networks use ARP to communicate with neighboring systems. The ARP protocol resolves an IP address to the MAC address of the destination system. Resolved addresses are stored in a cache which can be displayed using the **arp** command, as shown in the above example.

Common usage examples:

arp | Display the address resolution protocol cache

ping

Purpose: Send ICMP echo requests to network hosts.

Usage syntax: `ping [OPTIONS] [HOST]`

```
$ ping -c 5 10.10.1.1
PING 10.10.1.1 (10.10.1.1) 56(84) bytes of data.
64 bytes from 10.10.1.1: icmp_seq=1 ttl=64 time=0.286 ms
64 bytes from 10.10.1.1: icmp_seq=2 ttl=64 time=0.235 ms
64 bytes from 10.10.1.1: icmp_seq=3 ttl=64 time=0.232 ms
64 bytes from 10.10.1.1: icmp_seq=4 ttl=64 time=0.212 ms
64 bytes from 10.10.1.1: icmp_seq=5 ttl=64 time=0.216 ms
--- 10.10.1.1 ping statistics ---
5 packets transmitted, 5 received, 0% packet loss, time 4002ms
```

Using the ping command to ping a network host

The `ping` command sends ICMP echo requests to network hosts. This can be helpful when troubleshooting network connectivity problems. In the above example, executing `ping -c 5` sends five ping packets to the host with the IP address of 10.10.1.1.

Note	*If the `-c` parameter is omitted, the `ping` command will continue until interrupted (by pressing **CTRL + C**).*

Tip	*The `ping6` command is used to ping IP version 6 hosts.*

Common usage examples:

`ping [HOST]`	Ping the specified host
`ping -c [NUM] [HOST]`	Send the specified number of ICMP packets
`ping -f [HOST]`	Perform a rapid (flood) ping

traceroute

Purpose: Display TCP/IP routing information.

Usage syntax: traceroute [OPTIONS] [HOST]

```
$ traceroute -n www.google.com
traceroute to www.google.com (74.125.95.103), 30 hops max, 60 byte
packets
 1  192.168.1.254  3.634 ms  3.758 ms  4.511 ms
 2  99.60.32.2  25.398 ms  27.472 ms  28.040 ms
 3  76.196.172.4  28.261 ms  28.739 ms  28.926 ms
 4  151.164.94.52  29.057 ms  29.583 ms  29.824 ms
 5  69.220.8.57  39.645 ms  *  40.455 ms
 6  72.14.197.113  41.461 ms  39.534 ms  39.995 ms
 7  72.14.233.67  39.437 ms 72.14.233.65  31.567 ms  36.633 ms
 8  216.239.47.121  42.631 ms  43.298 ms 216.239.47.131  44.649 ms
...
```

Using traceroute to display the route of TCP/IP packets

The **traceroute** command traces the path that packets travel in TCP/IP networks. The above example demonstrates using the **traceroute** command to display the network route to www.google.com. Routers (AKA hops) along the network path are identified, along with a response time (in milliseconds).

Tip	The **traceroute6** command is used to trace IP version 6 hosts.

Common usage examples:

traceroute [HOST]	Trace the route to the specified host
traceroute -n [HOST]	Do not lookup DNS names when tracing

tracepath

Purpose: Display TCP/IP routing information on Linux systems.

Usage syntax: `tracepath [OPTIONS] [HOST]`

```
$ tracepath -n www.google.com
 1:  192.168.1.64      0.207ms pmtu 1500
 1:  192.168.1.254     1.482ms
 1:  192.168.1.254     1.263ms
 2:  99.60.32.2        27.476ms
 3:  76.196.172.4      27.227ms
 4:  151.164.94.52     27.428ms
 5:  69.220.8.57       37.468ms asymm  7
 6:  no reply
 7:  no reply
 8:  no reply
...
```

Using the tracepath command to display routing paths

The `tracepath` command is a replacement for the `traceroute` command on Linux systems. You can use either program on Linux, but many distributions only include `tracepath` by default. The above example demonstrates using `tracepath` to display the route to www.google.com.

> **Tip** The `tracepath6` *command is used to trace IP version 6 hosts.*

Common usage examples:

`tracepath [HOST]`	Trace the path to the specified host
`tracepath -n [HOST]`	Do not lookup DNS names when tracing

nslookup

Purpose: Perform DNS lookups on Unix systems.

Usage syntax: `nslookup [OPTIONS] [HOST]`

```
$ nslookup www.dontfearthecommandline.com
Server:         68.105.28.14
Address:        68.105.28.14#53

Non-authoritative answer:
Name:   dontfearthecommandline.com
Address: 64.202.189.170
```

Using the nslookup command to resolve a domain name

The `nslookup` command performs DNS lookup queries. It resolves DNS names to IP addresses and is helpful for troubleshooting network name resolution problems. In the above example, the IP address of the specified host is resolved and displayed.

Note	`nslookup` *is considered to be a legacy program and has been replaced by more modern commands such as* `dig` *(see page 161) and* `host` *(see page 162) on many systems.*

Common usage examples:

`nslookup [HOST]`	Resolve the specified host name

dig

Purpose: Perform DNS lookups on BSD and Linux systems.

Usage syntax: `dig [OPTIONS] [HOST]`

```
$ dig dontfearthecommandline.com
; <<>> DiG 9.5.1-P2 <<>> dontfearthecommandline.com
;; global options:  printcmd
;; Got answer:
;; ->>HEADER<<- opcode: QUERY, status: NOERROR, id: 20739
;; flags: qr rd ra; QUERY: 1, ANSWER: 1, AUTHORITY: 0, ADDITIONAL: 0

;; QUESTION SECTION:
;dontfearthecommandline.com.    IN      A

;; ANSWER SECTION:
dontfearthecommandline.com. 2681 IN    A       64.202.189.170

;; Query time: 4 msec
;; SERVER: 10.10.1.44#53(10.10.1.44)
;; WHEN: Mon Jun  1 05:38:40 2009
;; MSG SIZE  rcvd: 60
```

Typical output of the dig command

The `dig` command performs DNS queries on Linux and BSD systems. It is a modern replacement for the `nslookup` command. The above example demonstrates the typical usage of the `dig` command.

Common usage examples:

`dig [HOST]`	Display DNS information for the specified host
`dig -t MX [HOST]`	Display the mail server for the specified host
`dig -t NS [HOST]`	Display the name server for the specified host

host

Purpose: Simple DNS lookup utility.

Usage syntax: host [OPTIONS] [HOST]

```
$ host dontfearthecommandline.com
dontfearthecommandline.com has address 64.202.189.170
dontfearthecommandline.com mail is handled by 0 smtp.secureserver.net.
dontfearthecommandline.com mail is handled by 10
mailstore1.secureserver.net.
```

Resolving a name using the host command

The **host** command is a simple DNS lookup utility for Unix and Linux systems. It is similar to the **nslookup** and **dig** utilities, except it provides user friendly output that is easier to read and understand. The above example displays a sample of the output produced by the **host** command.

The **-t** option can be used with the **host** command to lookup other information about the domain such as the mail server (**-t MX**) and name server (**-t NS**) as shown in the next example.

```
$ host -t MX dontfearthecommandline.com
dontfearthecommandline.com mail is handled by 10
mailstore1.secureserver.net.
dontfearthecommandline.com mail is handled by 0 smtp.secureserver.net.
$ host -t NS dontfearthecommandline.com
dontfearthecommandline.com name server ns36.domaincontrol.com.
dontfearthecommandline.com name server ns35.domaincontrol.com.
```

Resolving MX and NS records using the host command

Common usage examples:

host [HOST]	Display DNS information for the specified host
host -t MX [HOST]	Display the mail server for the specified host
host -t NS [HOST]	Display the name server for the specified host
host -a [HOST]	Display detailed information for the specified host

whois

Purpose: Lookup domain name registry information in the WHOIS database.

Usage syntax: `whois [OPTIONS] [DOMAIN]`

```
$ whois google.com
Registrant:
        Dns Admin
        Google Inc.
        Please contact contact-admin@google.com
        1600 Amphitheatre Parkway
        Mountain View CA 94043
        dns-admin@google.com +1.650******* Fax: +1.650*******
    Domain Name: google.com
        Registrar Name: Markmonitor.com
        Registrar Whois: whois.markmonitor.com
        Registrar Homepage: http://www.markmonitor.com
    Created on.............: 1997-09-15.
    Expires on.............: 2011-09-13.
    Record last updated on..: 2008-06-08.
    Domain servers in listed order:
    ns1.google.com ns2.google.com
...
```
Using the whois command to query domain information

The `whois` command is used to query an internet registry and display information about the registrant of a domain name. In the above example, the `whois` command displays information for google.com.

	You can also use the `whois` command to lookup information about an IP address by executing `whois [IP ADDRESS]`.

Common usage examples:

`whois [DOMAIN]`	Display information about a domain's registrant
`whois [IP ADDRESS]`	Display information about the owner of an IP address

netstat

Purpose: Display network connections, statistics, and routing information.

Usage syntax: `netstat [OPTIONS]`

```
# netstat
Active Internet connections (w/o servers)
Proto Recv-Q Send-Q  Local Address       Foreign Address         State
tcp        0    463  10.10.2.4:110       12.185.92.178:50598     ESTABLISHED
tcp        0      0  10.10.2.4:110       66.103.123.134:1402     TIME_WAIT
tcp        0      0  127.0.0.1:10030     127.0.0.1:53041         ESTABLISHED
tcp        0      0  127.0.0.1:10025     127.0.0.1:38740         TIME_WAIT
tcp        0     72  10.10.2.4:22        10.10.1.251:50082       ESTABLISHED
...
```

Default output of the netstat command

netstat is a helpful utility that displays network status information. Executing **netstat** with no options will display all active network connections on the local system, as show in the above example. It can also be used to display detailed network statistics using the **-s** option, as shown in the next example.

```
# netstat -s
Ip:
    200104378 total packets received
    0 forwarded
    0 incoming packets discarded
    200104318 incoming packets delivered
    258439688 requests sent out
...
```

Using the -s option to display network statistics with netstat

The **-rn** option is another helpful feature that displays TCP/IP routing tables.

```
$ netstat -r
Kernel IP routing table
Destination  Gateway      Genmask          Flags  MSS Window  irtt Iface
10.10.2.0    0.0.0.0      255.255.255.0  U          0 0         0 eth0
0.0.0.0      10.10.2.1    0.0.0.0          UG         0 0         0 eth0
```

Displaying routing tables with netstat

Common usage examples:

`netstat`	Display active network connections
`netstat -s`	Display network statistics
`netstat -r`	Display routing information

route

Purpose: Display and configure TCP/IP routes.

Usage syntax: `route [OPTIONS]`

```
$ route -n
Kernel IP routing table
Destination      Gateway          Genmask          Flags Metric Ref  Use Iface
192.168.101.0    0.0.0.0          255.255.255.0    U     0      0      0 wlan0
10.10.1.0        0.0.0.0          255.255.255.0    U     0      0      0 eth0
0.0.0.0          10.10.1.1        0.0.0.0          UG    0      0      0 eth0
0.0.0.0          192.168.101.1    0.0.0.0          UG    0      0      0 wlan0
```
Displaying routing tables

The `route` command displays and configures network routes. In the above example, executing `route -n` displays the local system's routing table.

The `add` and `del` options can be used to add or delete static routes as shown in the next example.

```
# route add -net 10.10.2.0/24 gw 10.10.1.1 eth0
# route del -net 10.10.2.0/24
```
Adding and removing static TCP/IP routes

Common usage examples:

`route -n`	Display routing tables
`route add [ROUTE]`	Add the specified static route
`route del [ROUTE]`	Delete the specified static route

165

ifstat

Purpose: Display network interface statistics.

Usage syntax: `ifstat [DELAY] [COUNT]`

```
$ ifstat 2 10
      eth1
KB/s in   KB/s out
   0.02       0.04
   0.02       0.04
  10.68       0.86
  44.49       2.93
   3.45       7.95
   2.33      48.46
   0.40       0.86
   0.04       0.11
   3.26       0.58
   0.02       0.04
```

Displaying network interface statistics using ifstat

`ifstat` displays network interface statistics. It can be used to monitor network interface activity over a period of time. In the above example, executing `ifstat 2 10` displays interface statistics every two seconds for ten iterations.

Note	*If no arguments are specified, `ifstat` will continuously display network utilization until interrupted (by pressing **CTRL + C**).*

Common usage examples:

`ifstat`	Continuously display network utilization
`ifstat [DELAY]`	Update results at the specified interval
`ifstat [DELAY] [COUNT]`	End after reaching the specified count

tcpdump

Purpose: Displays raw traffic on a network interface.

Usage syntax: `tcpdump [OPTIONS]`

```
# tcpdump
listening on eth0, link-type EN10MB (Ethernet), capture size 96 bytes
05:59:05.027107 arp who-has 10.10.1.242 tell 1t-cad12-
01.dontfearthecommandline.com
05:59:05.028261 IP dt-office-27.dontfearthecommandline.com.50999 >
exchange-01.dontfearthecommandline.com.domain: 9454+ PTR?
242.1.10.10.in-addr.arpa. (42)
05:59:05.028459 arp who-has dt-office-27.dontfearthecommandline.com
tell exchange-01.dontfearthecommandline.com
05:59:05.028475 arp reply dt-office-27.dontfearthecommandline.com is-at
00:21:70:ac:f7:e7 (oui Unknown)
...
18 packets captured
303 packets received by filter
0 packets dropped by kernel
```

Using the tcpdump command to capture network traffic

`tcpdump` displays network packets sent and received to and from the local system. It can be helpful in monitoring network conditions or troubleshooting connectivity problems.

In the above example, **tcpdump** captures network traffic on the `eth0` interface. Information on each packet is then displayed on the screen. The capture will continue until interrupted (by pressing **CTRL + C**).

> **Tip**
>
> *Output from* `tcpdump` *can be difficult to interpret. A free utility called Wireshark is available that can be used to import* `tcpdump` *packet captures for easy viewing. Wireshark is available for Linux, Mac OS X, and Windows systems. Visit www.wireshark.com for more information.*

Common usage examples:

`tcpdump`	Display network traffic on the screen
`tcpdump > [FILE]`	Save the packet capture to a file
`tcpdump -i [INTERFACE]`	Capture traffic on the specified interface
`tcpdump -vv`	Display verbose packet information
`tcpdump -c [COUNT]`	Stop after receiving the specified number of packets

dhclient

Purpose: DHCP client for Linux and BSD systems.

Usage syntax: `dhclient [OPTIONS] [INTERFACE]`

```
# dhclient eth0
Listening on LPF/eth0/00:21:70:ac:f7:e7
Sending on   LPF/eth0/00:21:70:ac:f7:e7
Sending on   Socket/fallback
DHCPREQUEST of 10.10.1.100 on eth0 to 255.255.255.255 port 67
DHCPACK of 10.10.1.100 from 10.10.1.45
bound to 10.10.1.100 -- renewal in 37193 seconds.
```

Using dhclient to request a DHCP address

`dhclient` is a client for requesting an IP address from a DHCP server. The above example demonstrates using the `dhclient` command to request an IP address for the `eth0` interface.

Tip	*To release a DHCP address, execute* `dhclient -r` *on the command line.*

Common usage examples:

`dhclient [INTERFACE]`	Request an IP address from the DHCP server
`dhclient -r [INTERFACE]`	Release an assigned IP address

nmap

Purpose: Scan TCP/IP ports on network systems.

Usage syntax: `nmap [OPTIONS] [HOST]`

```
# nmap -O 10.10.1.70

Starting Nmap 5.00 ( http://nmap.org ) at 2010-05-06 16:55 CDT
Interesting ports on 10.10.1.70:
Not shown: 995 closed ports
PORT      STATE SERVICE
135/tcp   open  msrpc
139/tcp   open  netbios-ssn
445/tcp   open  microsoft-ds
5800/tcp  open  vnc-http
5900/tcp  open  vnc
MAC Address: 00:1A:A0:05:6B:19 (Dell)
Device type: general purpose
Running: Microsoft Windows XP
OS details: Microsoft Windows XP SP2 or SP3, or Windows Server 2003
Network Distance: 1 hop

OS detection performed. Please report any incorrect results at
http://nmap.org/submit/
Nmap done: 1 IP address (1 host up) scanned in 2.94 seconds
```

Using the nmap command to scan a network host

nmap is a network scanning utility. It can be used to evaluate security and troubleshoot network connectivity issues. In the above example, the **nmap** command is used to identify the operating system and open ports on the specified target host.

Tip	For the best results, use **nmap** as the root user or via the **sudo** command. This allows **nmap** to have access to have unrestricted access to system resources when performing network scans.

Common usage examples:

`nmap [HOST]`	Display open ports on the specified host
`nmap -PN [HOST]`	Do not ping the target before scanning
`nmap -O [HOST]`	Display the operating system of the target system
`nmap -A [HOST]`	Perform an aggressive scan

telnet

Purpose: Client for connecting to remote servers via the telnet protocol.

Usage syntax: `telnet [OPTIONS] [HOST]`

```
$ telnet myserver
login: nick
password: ******
$
```

Connecting to a remote system using the telnet command

The `telnet` command is used to connect to remote systems via the telnet protocol. The above example demonstrates connecting to a remote system using `telnet`. Once connected to the remote system you can execute commands as if you were logged into the system locally.

Note	*Telnet is an insecure legacy protocol and has largely been replaced by SSH for security reasons. Usernames, passwords, and other sensitive information transmitted via telnet are sent in plain text making it very easy for hackers to capture. Avoid using telnet whenever possible, especially when communicating over untrusted networks such as the internet.*

Common usage examples:

`telnet [HOST]` | Start a telnet session to a remote system

ssh

Purpose: Client for connecting to remote servers via the SSH protocol.

Usage syntax: ssh [OPTIONS] [HOST]

```
$ ssh myserver
nick@myserver's password: ******
$
```

Using the ssh command to connect to a remote system

The **ssh** command is used to connect to remote systems via the SSH protocol. SSH creates an encrypted connection between two systems and provides a secure channel for communication. This helps prevent "man in the middle" hackers from being able to capture sensitive information (such as usernames and passwords) when connecting to remote systems.

Tip	*PuTTY, a free SSH and telnet client for Windows, can be downloaded at www.chiark.greenend.org.uk/~sgtatham/putty/. This allows you to connect to remote Unix, Linux, and BSD servers directly from Windows systems.*

Common usage examples:

ssh [HOST]	Start an SSH session to a remote system
ssh -l [USER] [HOST]	Login as the specified user on the target system
ssh -C [HOST]	Enable compression (for slow connections)

minicom

Purpose: Serial communication application.

Usage syntax: `minicom [OPTIONS]`

```
$ minicom
Welcome to minicom 2.3

OPTIONS: I18n
Compiled on Sep 25 2009, 23:40:20.
Port /dev/ttyS0


          Press CTRL-A Z for help on special keys


cisco-router>
```

Using minicom to connect to a serial console device

`minicom` is a serial communication utility for BSD and Linux systems. It can be used to connect to serial devices (like routers and switches) via the command line. The example above demonstrates using `minicom` to connect to a serial attached Cisco router.

> **Tip**
> Press **CTRL + A** then **Z** *for a* `minicom` *help summary. To exit* `minicom`, *press* **CTRL + A** then **X**.

Common usage examples:

`minicom`	Connect to the default serial device
`minicom -s`	Edit minicom settings

mail

Purpose: Send email to local and remote users.

Usage syntax: `mail [OPTIONS] [ADDRESS]`

```
$ mail grepnick@gmail.com
Subject: Hello
Want to go get some tacos?
<CTRL + D>
```
Sending an email message with the mail command

The `mail` command sends email messages. In the above example, a new email message is created and addressed to the specified recipient. After pressing enter, the mail client will prompt you for a subject for the message. Pressing enter again will start the body of the message. Pressing **CTRL + D** exits the mail client and sends the message.

Tip	Press **CTRL + C** twice to cancel editing and discard a mail message (without sending).

A text file can be substituted for the body of an email message. In the next example, the text in the `message.txt` file will be sent as the body of the message.

```
$ mail -s "Hello" grepnick@gmail.com < message.txt
```
Using a text file as a message body

Common usage examples:

`mail`	Check for new email
`mail [ADDRESS]`	Start a new message to the specified address
`mail [ADDRESS] < [FILE]`	Use the specified file as the message body
`mail -s "[SUBJECT]" \` `[ADDRESS]`	Specify a message subject on the command line

ftp

Purpose: Transfer files using FTP (**F**ile **T**ransfer **P**rotocol).

Usage syntax: `ftp [OPTIONS] [HOST]`

```
# ftp 10.10.1.48
Connected to 10.10.1.48.
Name (10.10.1.48): nick
Password: ********
230 Login successful.
Remote system type is UNIX.
Using binary mode to transfer files.
ftp>
```

Connecting to an FTP server using the ftp command

The `ftp` command transfers files using the FTP protocol. The above example demonstrates using the `ftp` command to connect to a remote FTP server. Once connected to the remote system, you can execute one of the FTP shell commands listed in the following table.

Command	Function
`ascii`	Transfer files in ASCII format
`binary`	Transfer files in binary format
`status`	Display the connection status
`pwd`	Print the current working directory
`ls`	List remote directory contents
`get [FILE]`	Download the specified remote file
`put [FILE]`	Upload the specified local file
`cd [PATH]`	Change directories on the remote system
`lcd [PATH]`	Change directories on the local system
`mkdir [DIR]`	Create a directory
`rmdir [DIR]`	Remove a directory
`delete [FILE]`	Remove a file
`rename [FILE]`	Rename a file
`bye`	Terminate the FTP connection

FTP commands

Common usage examples:

`ftp [HOST]`	Start an FTP session with the specified host
`ftp -p [HOST]`	Use passive mode for data transfers

174

wget

Purpose: File download utility for Linux systems.

Usage syntax: `wget [OPTIONS] [SOURCE]`

```
$ wget http://kernel.org/pub/linux/kernel/v2.6/patch-2.6.29.4.bz2
--2009-06-02 01:15:58--  http://kernel.org/pub/linux/kernel/v2.6/patch-
2.6.29.4.bz2
Resolving kernel.org... 149.20.20.133, 204.152.191.37
Connecting to kernel.org|149.20.20.133|:80... connected.
HTTP request sent, awaiting response... 200 OK
Length: 91866 (90K) [application/x-bzip2]
Saving to: 'patch-2.6.29.4.bz2'
100%[====================================>] 91,866  99.6K/s  in 0.9s
2009-06-02 01:16:03 (99.6 KB/s) - 'patch-2.6.29.4.bz2' saved
```

Downloading a file from the internet with the wget command

`wget` is a file download utility for the command line. It can be used to download files via HTTP and FTP protocols. In the above example, a file is downloaded from a remote HTTP system and saved in the current directory.

Tip	*Use the* `--user=[USERNAME]` *and* `--password=[PASSWORD]` *options to specify a username and password to used when connecting to the remote system.*

Common usage examples:

`wget http://[HOST/FILE]`	Download the specified file via HTTP
`wget ftp://[HOST/FILE]`	Download the specified file via FTP

showmount

Purpose: Display NFS mount and export information.

Usage syntax: `showmount [OPTIONS]`

```
# showmount
Hosts on noc-01:
10.10.1.48
```
Displaying connected NFS clients using the showmount command

The `showmount` command displays information about an NFS server running on the local system. The above example demonstrates using `showmount` to display a list of clients currently connected to the NFS server.

The next example demonstrates using the `-e` option to display the NFS server's export list.

```
# showmount -e
Export list for noc-01:
/home 10.10.1.0/255.255.255.0
```
Displaying a list of exported directories

The `-d` option is used to display a list of exported directories that are currently in use, as shown in the next example.

```
# showmount -d
Directories on noc-01:
/home
```
Displaying a list of exported directories that are currently in use

Common usage examples:

`showmount`	Display NFS clients currently connected to the server
`showmount -e`	Display the NFS server's exported directories
`showmount -d`	List exported directories that are currently in use
`showmount -a`	Display NFS clients and the directories they have mounted

Section 9: Hardware Management Commands

Overview

Commands in this section cover basic Unix, Linux, and BSD hardware management utilities. These commands can be used to identify, configure, and troubleshoot system devices.

Commands covered in this section:

Command	Purpose
lshw	List hardware on Linux systems.
ioscan	List hardware on HP-UX systems.
lsdev	List hardware on AIX systems.
lspci	List PCI devices on Linux systems.
pciconf	List PCI devices on BSD systems.
lsusb	List USB devices on Linux systems.
dmidecode	Display detailed information about devices on the system.
hdparm	Display/set hard drive parameters on Linux systems.
eject	Unload removable media.

Glossary of terms used in this section:

IDE   (Integrated Drive Electronics) Legacy interface used to link disk drives to a computer.

PCI   (Peripheral Component Interconnect) Interface used to connect internal devices to a computer.

SATA   (Serial Advanced Technology Attachment) Modern interface used to link disk drives to a computer.

USB   (Universal Serial Bus) Interface used to connect external devices to a computer.

lshw

Purpose: List hardware on Linux systems.

Usage syntax: `lshw [OPTIONS]`

```
# lshw -short
H/W path            Device  Class       Description
===================================================================
                            system      OptiPlex GX520
/0                          bus         0WG233
/0/0                        memory      64KiB BIOS
/0/400                      processor   Intel(R) Pentium(R) 4 CPU 3.00GHz
/0/400/700                  memory      16KiB L1 cache
/0/400/701                  memory      2MiB L2 cache
/0/400/0.1                  processor   Logical CPU
/0/400/0.2                  processor   Logical CPU
/0/1000                     memory      2GiB System Memory
/0/1000/0                   memory      1GiB DIMM DDR Synchronous 533 MHz
. . .
```

Output of the lshw command using the -short option

The `lshw` command lists information about all hardware installed on Linux systems. In the above example, the `-short` option is used to provide a simple listing of hardware detected on the local system. Omitting the `-short` option will display a detailed listing of devices, as demonstrated in the next example.

```
# lshw
noc-01
    description: Mini Tower Computer
    product: OptiPlex GX520
    vendor: Dell Inc.
    serial: *******
    width: 32 bits
    capabilities: smbios-2.3 dmi-2.3 smp-1.4 smp
    configuration: administrator_password=enabled boot=normal
chassis=mini-tower cpus=1
  *-core
      description: Motherboard
      product: 0WG233
      vendor: Dell Inc.
. . .
```

Default output of the lshw command

Common usage examples:

`lshw`	Display a detailed hardware listing
`lshw -short`	Display a simple hardware listing

ioscan

Purpose: List hardware on HP-UX systems.

Usage syntax: `ioscan [OPTIONS]`

```
# ioscan
H/W Path    Class                     Description
===================================================
            bc
8           bc                        I/O Adapter
8/0              ext_bus              GSC add-on Fast/Wide SCSI Interface
8/0.5               target
8/0.5.0                disk           SEAGATE ST34371W
8/0.7               target
8/0.7.0                ctl            Initiator
8/0.8               target
8/0.8.0                disk           SEAGATE ST318436LC
8/4         ba                        PCI Bus Bridge - GSCtoPCI
8/4/1/0          lan                  HP J3515A HSC 10/100Base-TX D-Class
1 port
8/16        ba                        Core I/O Adapter
8/16/0           ext_bus              Built-in Parallel Interface
8/16/4           tty                  Built-in RS-232C
8/16/5           ext_bus              Built-in SCSI
8/16/5.0            target
8/16/5.0.0             tape           HP       C1537A
8/16/5.2            target
8/16/5.2.0             disk           SONY     CD-ROM CDU-76S
8/16/5.7            target
8/16/5.7.0             ctl            Initiator
8/16/6           lan                  Built-in LAN
8/16/7           ps2                  Built-in Keyboard/Mouse
8/20        ba                        Core I/O Adapter
8/20/2           tty                  Built-in RS-232C
...
```

Listing devices with ioscan on HP-UX

`ioscan` displays information about hardware installed on HP-UX systems. The above example displays the typical output of this command which shows information about the system's hardware profile.

Common usage examples:

`ioscan`	Display a simple hardware listing
`ioscan -f`	Display a detailed hardware listing

lsdev

Purpose: List hardware on AIX systems.

Usage syntax: `lsdev [OPTIONS]`

```
# lsdev
L2cache0    Available             L2 Cache
cd0         Available 1G-19-00    IDE DVD-ROM Drive
en0         Available 1L-08       Standard Ethernet Network Interface
en1         Defined   1j-08       Standard Ethernet Network Interface
ent0        Available 1L-08       10/100 Mbps Ethernet PCI Adapter II
ent1        Available 1j-08       10/100/1000 Base-TX PCI-X Adapter
et0         Defined   1L-08       IEEE 802.3 Ethernet Network Interface
et1         Defined   1j-08       IEEE 802.3 Ethernet Network Interface
fd0         Available 01-D1-00-00 Diskette Drive
fda0        Available 01-D1       Standard I/O Diskette Adapter
hd1         Defined               Logical volume
hd2         Defined               Logical volume
hd3         Defined               Logical volume
hd4         Defined               Logical volume
hd5         Defined               Logical volume
hd6         Defined               Logical volume
hd8         Defined               Logical volume
hd10opt     Defined               Logical volume
hd11admin   Defined               Logical volume
hd9var      Defined               Logical volume
hdisk0      Available 1S-08-00-5,0 16 Bit LVD SCSI Disk Drive
hdisk1      Defined   1S-08-00-8,0 Other SCSI Disk Drive
hdisk2      Available 1S-08-00-8,0 16 Bit LVD SCSI Disk Drive
ide0        Available 1G-19        ATA/IDE Controller Device
...
```

Listing devices on AIX with lsdev

`lsdev` displays information about hardware installed on AIX systems. The above example displays the typical output of this command which includes information about hardware installed on the local system.

Common usage examples:

`lsdev` | Display a simple hardware listing

lspci

Purpose: List PCI devices on Linux systems.

Usage syntax: `lspci [OPTIONS]`

```
# lspci
00:00.0 Host bridge: Intel Corporation 82945G/GZ/P/PL Memory Controller
Hub (rev 02)
00:01.0 PCI bridge: Intel Corporation 82945G/GZ/P/PL PCI Express Root
Port (rev 02)
00:02.0 VGA compatible controller: Intel Corporation 82945G/GZ
Integrated Graphics Controller (rev 02)
00:02.1 Display controller: Intel Corporation 82945G/GZ Integrated
Graphics Controller (rev 02)
00:1c.0 PCI bridge: Intel Corporation 82801G (ICH7 Family) PCI Express
Port 1 (rev 01)
00:1c.1 PCI bridge: Intel Corporation 82801G (ICH7 Family) PCI Express
Port 2 (rev 01)
...
```

Displaying a PCI device listing using the lspci command

`lspci` lists PCI devices on Linux systems. In the above example, a basic PCI device list is displayed. A more detailed listing can be produced by using the `-v` option as demonstrated in the next example.

```
# lspci -v
00:00.0 Host bridge: Intel Corporation 82945G/GZ/P/PL Memory Controller
Hub (rev 02)
        Subsystem: Dell Device 01ad
        Flags: bus master, fast devsel, latency 0
        Capabilities: [e0] Vendor Specific Information <?>
        Kernel driver in use: agpgart-intel
        Kernel modules: intel-agp

00:01.0 PCI bridge: Intel Corporation 82945G/GZ/P/PL PCI Express Root
Port (rev 02)
        Flags: bus master, fast devsel, latency 0
        Bus: primary=00, secondary=01, subordinate=01, sec-latency=0
        Memory behind bridge: fe900000-fe9fffff
        Capabilities: [88] Subsystem: Intel Corporation Device 0000
        Capabilities: [80] Power Management version 2
...
```

Displaying a verbose PCI device listing

Common usage examples:

`lspci`	Display a simple PCI device list
`lspci -v`	Display a detailed PCI device list

pciconf

Purpose: List PCI devices on BSD systems.

Usage syntax: `pciconf [OPTIONS]`

```
# pciconf -lv | less
hostb0@pci0:0:0:0:      class=0x060000 card=0x00000000 chip=0x12378086
rev=0x02 hdr=0x00
    vendor    = 'Intel Corporation'
    device    = '82440/1FX 440FX (Natoma) System Controller'
    class     = bridge
    subclass  = HOST-PCI
isab0@pci0:0:1:0:       class=0x060100 card=0x00000000 chip=0x70008086
rev=0x00 hdr=0x00
    vendor    = 'Intel Corporation'
    device    = 'PIIX3 PCI-to-ISA Bridge (Triton II) (82371SB)'
    class     = bridge
    subclass  = PCI-ISA
atapci0@pci0:0:1:1:     class=0x01018a card=0x00000000 chip=0x71118086
rev=0x01 hdr=0x00
    vendor    = 'Intel Corporation'
    device    = 'PIIX4/4E/4M IDE Controller (82371AB/EB/MB)'
    class     = mass storage
    subclass  = ATA
vgapci0@pci0:0:2:0:     class=0x030000 card=0x00000000 chip=0xbeef80ee
...
```

Output of the pciconf command

The `pciconf` command displays PCI devices on BSD systems. The above example demonstrates listing PCI devices on a BSD system.

> **Note** The `pcidump` *or* `devinfo` *commands may be used on some BSD systems in place of the* `pciconf` *command.*

Common usage examples:

`pciconf -lv` Display a complete list of PCI devices

lsusb

Purpose: List USB devices on Linux systems.

Usage syntax: `lsusb [OPTIONS]`

```
# lsusb
Bus 003 Device 001: ID 1d6b:0001 Linux Foundation 1.1 root hub
Bus 004 Device 001: ID 1d6b:0001 Linux Foundation 1.1 root hub
Bus 001 Device 004: ID 0930:6544 Kingston DataTraveler 2.0 Stick (2GB)
Bus 001 Device 001: ID 1d6b:0002 Linux Foundation 2.0 root hub
Bus 005 Device 001: ID 1d6b:0001 Linux Foundation 1.1 root hub
Bus 002 Device 003: ID 0461:4d15 Dell Optical Mouse
Bus 002 Device 002: ID 413c:2105 Dell Model L100 Keyboard
Bus 002 Device 001: ID 1d6b:0001 Linux Foundation 1.1 root hub
```
Displaying a USB device listing using lsusb

`lsusb` lists USB devices on Linux systems. Executing `lsusb` with no options will display a simple listing of all USB devices on the local system, as shown in the above example.

The `-v` option can be used with `lsusb` to display a verbose listing of USB devices as shown in the next example.

```
# lsusb -v | less

Bus 003 Device 001: ID 1d6b:0001 Linux Foundation 1.1 root hub
Device Descriptor:
  bLength                18
  bDescriptorType         1
  bcdUSB               1.10
  bDeviceClass            9 Hub
  bDeviceSubClass         0 Unused
  bDeviceProtocol         0 Full speed (or root) hub
  bMaxPacketSize0        64
  idVendor           0x1d6b Linux Foundation
  idProduct          0x0001 1.1 root hub
  bcdDevice            2.06
...
```
Displaying a detailed USB device list

Common usage examples:

`lsusb`	Display USB devices
`lsusb -v`	Display a detailed list of USB devices
`lsusb -t`	Display USB devices in tree mode

dmidecode

Purpose: Display detailed information about devices on the system.

Usage syntax: `dmidecode [OPTIONS]`

```
# dmidecode
SMBIOS 2.31 present.
45 structures occupying 1654 bytes.
Table at 0x000E0010.

Handle 0x0000, DMI type 0, 20 bytes
BIOS Information
        Vendor: Phoenix Technologies LTD
        Version: 6.00
        Release Date: 04/17/2006
        Address: 0xE7C70
        Runtime Size: 99216 bytes
        ROM Size: 64 kB
        Characteristics:
                ISA is supported
                PCI is supported
                PC Card (PCMCIA) is supported
                PNP is supported
                APM is supported
                BIOS is upgradeable
                BIOS shadowing is allowed
                ESCD support is available
                USB legacy is supported
                Smart battery is supported
                BIOS boot specification is supported

Handle 0x0001, DMI type 1, 25 bytes
System Information
        Manufacturer: VMware, Inc.
        Product Name: VMware Virtual Platform
        Version: None
...
```

Displaying a list of devices in tree view

`dmidecode` displays a detailed list of devices on the system. The above example demonstrates the typical output of this command which includes verbose information about the system's hardware.

Tip	*The output of the* `dmidecode` *command can be quite lengthy. Typing* `dmidecode|more` *will display the output one page at a time.*

Common usage examples:

`dmidecode` | Display detailed information about devices on the system

hdparm

Purpose: Display/set hard drive parameters on Linux systems.

Usage syntax: `hdparm [OPTIONS] [DEVICE]`

```
# hdparm /dev/sda
/dev/sda:
 IO_support   =  0 (default)
 readonly     =  0 (off)
 readahead    = 6144 (on)
 geometry     = 19457/255/63, sectors = 312581808, start = 0
```
Typical output of the hdparm command

The `hdparm` command displays and edits hard drive settings. The example above displays the specified drive's settings. The fields displayed will vary depending on the type of drive in use.

> **Note**
>
> The `hdparm` command has dozens of options that can be used to modify disk drive settings. The options available depend on the type of drive being used (IDE, SATA, etc.). See `man hdparm` for more information and warnings specific to each option.

The `hdparm` command can also be used as a performance benchmark for disk drives using the `-Tt` option as displayed in the next example.

```
# hdparm -Tt /dev/sda

/dev/sda:
 Timing cached reads:    11832 MB in  1.99 seconds = 5932.95 MB/sec
 Timing buffered disk reads:  582 MB in  4.30 seconds = 135.30 MB/sec
```
Using the -Tt option to display disk performance benchmarks

Common usage examples:

`hdparm [DISK]`	Display settings for the specified disk
`hdparm -Tt [DISK]`	Display performance information for the specified disk

eject

Purpose: Unload removable media.

Usage syntax: `eject [OPTIONS] [DEVICE]`

```
# eject
```

Using the eject command to remove a CD or DVD

The `eject` command unloads removable media devices. It is primarily used to unmount and eject a CD or DVD. On most systems, simply typing the `eject` command will unmount and eject the tray on the disc drive.

> **Note** *Some systems may require you to specify which device to eject, such as* `eject /dev/cdrom`.

The `-v` option can be used with the `eject` command to display verbose messages when ejecting removable media as shown in the next example.

```
# eject -v /dev/cdrom
eject: device name is '/dev/cdrom'
eject: expanded name is '/dev/cdrom'
eject: '/dev/cdrom' is a link to '/dev/sr0'
eject: '/dev/sr0' is mounted at '/media/FOTC_S2_DISC1'
eject: unmounting device '/dev/sr0' from '/media/FOTC_S2_DISC1'
eject: '/dev/sr0' is not a multipartition device
eject: trying to eject '/dev/sr0' using CD-ROM eject command
eject: CD-ROM eject command succeeded
```

Displaying verbose messages with the eject -v command

Common usage examples:

`eject`	Eject the default removable device
`eject [DEVICE]`	Eject the specified device
`eject -c [SLOT] [DEVICE]`	Eject a specific slot on a CD changer device
`eject -v`	Display verbose messages

Section 10: File Systems

Overview

This section covers usage of basic file system management commands. It also covers popular partition editors for Unix, Linux, and BSD systems such as `fdisk` and `parted`. These commands can be used to create, modify, and delete file systems.

Warning	*The following commands can cause irreparable damage to your system if used incorrectly. Always experiment with new commands in a testing environment.*

Commands covered in this section:

Command	Purpose
`fdisk`	Display and edit hard disk partitions.
`parted`	Display and edit partitions on Linux systems.
`mkfs`	Create file systems.
`fsck`	Check and repair file systems.
`badblocks`	Check a disk drive for bad blocks.
`tune2fs`	Adjust Linux file system parameters.
`mount` `umount`	Mount/unmount local and remote file systems.
`mkswap`	Create swap space storage.
`swapon` `swapoff`	Activate/deactivate swap space.
`swapinfo`	Display swap space information.
`sync`	Flush file system buffers.

Glossary of terms used in this section:

Blocks	Physical storage units on a disk drive.
File System	A method and format for storing data on a disk drive.
Format	The process of preparing a disk drive for a specific file system.
Mount	Process used to attach storage devices to a local system.
Partition	A division of a disk drive.
Swap	A file or partition that acts as secondary storage for RAM.

fdisk

Purpose: Display and edit hard disk partitions.

Usage syntax: `fdisk [OPTIONS] [DEVICE]`

```
# fdisk -l /dev/sda
Disk /dev/sda: 160.0 GB, 1600418'696 bytes
255 heads, 63 sectors/track, 19457 cylinders
Units = cylinders of 16065 * 512 = 8225280 bytes
Disk identifier: 0x98000000

   Device Boot      Start         End      Blocks   Id  System
/dev/sda1   *           1          12       96358+  de  Dell Utility
/dev/sda2              13       19457   156191962+   5  Extended
/dev/sda5              13         504     3951958+  82  Linux swap / Solaris
/dev/sda6             505       19457   152239941   83  Linux
```

Listing the partitions on a disk using the fdisk command

fdisk is a disk partition editor for Unix, Linux, and BSD systems. In the above example, the `-l` option is used to display the partition information for the specified hard disk.

Executing **fdisk** with no options will open the specified disk for editing, as displayed in the next example.

```
# fdisk /dev/sda
Command (m for help): p

Disk /dev/sda: 160.0 GB, 160041885696 bytes
255 heads, 63 sectors/track, 19457 cylinders
Units = cylinders of 16065 * 512 = 8225280 bytes
Disk identifier: 0x98000000

   Device Boot      Start         End      Blocks   Id  System
/dev/sda1   *           1          12       96358+  de  Dell Utility
/dev/sda2              13       19457   156191962+   5  Extended
/dev/sda5              13         504     3951958+  82  Linux swap / Solaris
/dev/sda6             505       19457   152239941   83  Linux
```

Using the fdisk utility to modify a partition

In this example, the **fdisk** utility starts an interactive shell that can be used to display and modify a disk's partitions. Within the shell, command keys are used to perform a specific task. The following table describes the basic commands available within the **fdisk** utility.

(Continued...)

Command	Function
m	Display the help menu
p	Display the partition table
n	Create a new partition
a	Make a partition bootable
d	Delete a partition
l	List partition types
q	Quit without saving changes
w	Save changes and exit

Basic fdisk commands

Warning	*Incorrectly using the* `fdisk` *utility can cause data loss or leave your system unbootable. Always use caution when editing disk partitions and make sure to have a backup of your important data.*

Common usage examples:

`fdisk -l`	List the partition tables for all devices
`fdisk -l [DEVICE]`	List the partition tables on the specified device
`fdisk [DEVICE]`	Open the specified device for editing

parted

Purpose: Display and edit partitions on Linux systems.

Usage syntax: `parted [OPTIONS] [DEVICE]`

```
# parted -l /dev/sda
Model: ATA SAMSUNG HD080HJ/ (scsi)
Disk /dev/sda: 80.0GB
Sector size (logical/physical): 512B/512B
Partition Table: msdos

Number  Start    End     Size    Type      File system    Flags
 1      1049kB   106MB   105MB   primary   ntfs           boot
 2      106MB    47.2GB  47.1GB  primary   ntfs
 3      47.2GB   80.0GB  32.8GB  extended
 5      47.2GB   78.6GB  31.4GB  logical   ext4
 6      78.6GB   80.0GB  1398MB  logical   linux-swap(v1)
```
Displaying the partition layout of a disk using the parted utility

`parted` is a disk partition manager for Linux systems. It is similar to the `fdisk` utility (which is also available for Linux), except it offers a more user friendly interface. In the above example, the `-l` option is used to display the partition information for the specified hard disk.

Executing `parted` with no options will open the specified disk for editing, as displayed in the next example.

```
# parted /dev/sda
GNU Parted 1.8.8.1.159-1e0e
Using /dev/sda
Welcome to GNU Parted! Type 'help' to view a list of commands.
(parted) print
Model: ATA SAMSUNG HD080HJ/ (scsi)
Disk /dev/sda: 80.0GB
Sector size (logical/physical): 512B/512B
Partition Table: msdos

Number  Start    End     Size    Type      File system    Flags
 1      1049kB   106MB   105MB   primary   ntfs           boot
 2      106MB    47.2GB  47.1GB  primary   ntfs
 3      47.2GB   80.0GB  32.8GB  extended
 5      47.2GB   78.6GB  31.4GB  logical   ext4
 6      78.6GB   80.0GB  1398MB  logical   linux-swap(v1)
```
Editing a disk's partition using the parted utility

(Continued...)

The following table provides an overview of basic **parted** partition editing commands.

Command	Function
print	Display the partition table
help	Display the help menu
mkpart	Create a new partition
rm	Delete a partition
quit	Exit the program

Basic parted commands

Common usage examples:

parted -l	List the partition tables for all devices
parted -l [DEVICE]	List the partition tables on the specified device
parted [DEVICE]	Open the specified device for editing

mkfs

Purpose: Create file systems.

Usage syntax: mkfs [OPTIONS] [DEVICE]

```
# mkfs -t ext4 /dev/sdb1
mke2fs 1.41.9 (22-Aug-2009)
Filesystem label=
OS type: Linux
Block size=4096 (log=2)
Fragment size=4096 (log=2)
122400 inodes, 489131 blocks
24456 blocks (5.00%) reserved for the super user
First data block=0
Maximum file system blocks=503316480
15 block groups
32768 blocks per group, 32768 fragments per group
8160 inodes per group
Superblock backups stored on blocks:
        32768, 98304, 163840, 229376, 294912

Writing inode tables: done
Creating journal (8192 blocks): done
Writing superblocks and file system accounting information: done

This file system will be automatically checked every 21 mounts or
180 days, whichever comes first.  Use tune2fs -c or -i to override.
```

Creating an ext4 formatted file system using the mkfs command

The **mkfs** command creates (AKA formats) a file system on a disk drive. In the above example, the **mkfs** command is used on a Linux system to format the first partition of the /dev/sdb disk drive.

> **Warning** *The **mkfs** command will destroy all data on the target device.*

> **Note** *Usage syntax and supported options for **mkfs** vary across the different Unix, Linux, and BSD platforms. The above example was created on a Linux system. See **man mkfs** to find the correct usage syntax for your system.*

Common usage examples:

mkfs -t [FSTYPE] [DEVICE]	Create a file system on the specified drive
mkfs -ct [FSTYPE] [DEVICE]	Check for bad blocks before formatting

fsck

Purpose: Check and repair file systems.

Usage syntax: `fsck [OPTIONS] [FILESYSTEM]`

```
# fsck -n /
fsck 1.40.8 (13-Mar-2008)
e2fsck 1.40.8 (13-Mar-2008)
/dev/sda1 contains a file system with errors, check forced.
Pass 1: Checking inodes, blocks, and sizes
Pass 2: Checking directory structure
Pass 3: Checking directory connectivity
Pass 4: Checking reference counts
Pass 5: Checking group summary information
...
```

Using the fsck command to check a file system

`fsck` checks the specified file systems for errors and repairs them if necessary. In the above example, the / file system is checked for errors. The -n option is used to instruct `fsck` to check but not repair the specified file system. This is necessary since, in this case, the / file system is a live (mounted) file system and cannot be repaired unless first unmounted.

Warning	The `fsck` command should never be used to repair a mounted file system as it will cause data corruption. In Linux, you can safely run `fsck` at the next reboot by typing **sudo touch /forcefsck** on the command line. Other systems may require booting recovery media in order to use `fsck`. See **man fsck** for more information about usage on your system.

Common usage examples:

`fsck [FILESYSTEM]`	Check and repair the specified file system
`fsck -n [FILESYSTEM]`	Check the specified file system without repairing it

badblocks

Purpose: Check a disk drive for bad blocks.

Usage syntax: `badblocks [OPTIONS] [DEVICE]`

```
# badblocks -v /dev/sda
Checking blocks 0 to 8388607
Checking for bad blocks (read-only test): done
Pass completed, 0 bad blocks found.
```

Checking a device for bad blocks using the badblocks command

The **badblocks** command is a Linux utility used to search a disk drive for bad blocks. In the above example, the **badblocks** command is used to check /dev/sda for bad blocks. The **-v** option is included to display verbose status information during the scan.

A disk drive that is healthy should have no bad blocks. If bad blocks are found, the drive should be replaced immediately to avoid data loss.

Warning	*The default* **badblocks** *test is read-only and generally safe to use on a live file system. Specifying the* **-w** *option will perform a read/write test and will <u>destroy all data</u> on the specified disk. It should only be used to test a disk that does not contain critical data, as it will be completely overwritten.*

Common usage examples:

`badblocks [DEVICE]`	Check the specified device for bad blocks
`badblocks -v [DEVICE]`	Display verbose messages when checking
`badblocks -w [DEVICE]`	Perform a read/write test on the disk

tune2fs

Purpose: Adjust Linux file system parameters.

Usage syntax: `tune2fs [OPTIONS] [DEVICE]`

```
# tune2fs -l /dev/sda5
tune2fs 1.41.9 (22-Aug-2009)
Filesystem volume name:    <none>
Last mounted on:           /
Filesystem UUID:           68df1b51-492b-489a-80d8-0623900de3ba
Filesystem magic number:   0xEF53
Filesystem revision #:     1 (dynamic)
Filesystem features:       has_journal ext_attr resize_inode dir_index
filetype needs_recovery extent flex_bg sparse_super large_file
Filesystem flags:          signed_directory_hash
Default mount options:     (none)
Filesystem state:          clean
...
```

Displaying a file system's parameters using the tune2fs command

The `tune2fs` command displays and edits file system settings on Linux systems. It supports the ext2, ext3, and ext4 file systems. In the above example, the `-l` parameter is used to display detailed information about the specified file system.

`tune2fs` is most commonly used to adjust the `fsck` intervals for a file system. This is the interval in which the system will automatically run an `fsck` on the file system. The next example displays the variables that control this.

```
# tune2fs -l /dev/sda5 | grep -Ei 'check|max'
Maximum mount count:      32
Last checked:             Wed Mar 24 14:14:20 2010
Check interval:           15552000 (6 months)
Next check after:         Mon Sep 20 14:14:20 2010
```

Displaying a file system's fsck parameters

Common usage examples:

`tune2fs -l [device]`	Display information about the specified file system
`tune2fs -c [count] \ [device]`	Force the `fsck` command to check the file system after the specified number of mounts
`tune2fs -i [interval] \ [device]`	Force the `fsck` command to check the file system at the specified interval in days, weeks, or months

mount / umount

Purpose: Mount local and remote file systems.

Usage syntax: `mount [OPTIONS] [SOURCE] [TARGET]`

```
# mount /dev/sb1 /mnt/Seagate
```
Mounting a local file system

The `mount` command mounts file systems. In the above example, the device `/dev/sdb1` is mounted under the `/mnt/Seagate` directory. This is an example of mounting a local file system.

> **Tip** *Local file systems can be configured to mount automatically at boot using the* `/etc/fstab` *file.*

`mount` can also be used to mount remote file systems via NFS, as shown in the next example.

```
# mount 10.10.1.48:/home/nick /mnt/nick
```
Mounting an NFS file system

In this example, `/home/nick` on the remote machine (10.10.1.48) is shared via NFS and mounted locally in `/mnt/nick`.

> **Note** *NFS must be properly configured on the remote system for this to work. NFS settings are managed via the* `/etc/exports` *file.*

The `umount` command unmounts file systems as shown in the next example.

Usage syntax: `umount [OPTIONS] [DIRECTORY]`

```
# umount /mnt/Seagate
```
Unmounting a file system

Common usage examples:

`mount`	Display all mounted file systems
`mount [DEVICE] [DIR]`	Mount the specified device
`mount [IP]:[REMOTE] [LOCAL]`	Mount the specified NFS share
`umount [PATH]`	Unmount a file system

mkswap

Purpose: Create swap space storage.

Usage syntax: `mkswap [OPTIONS] [DEVICE]`

```
# mkswap /dev/sdb1
Setting up swapspace version 1, size = 522076 KiB
no label, UUID=cc35b16c-985f-4723-a5c4-e4dd2377aad
```
Creating swap storage using the mkswap command

The `mkswap` command creates swap space on Linux systems. Swap storage is used to store data in memory that is rarely accessed. This frees up RAM for active programs. In the above example, the `mkswap` command is used to create swap storage on the `/dev/sdb1` partition.

Tip	*Swap utilization has a significant impact on system performance. If a system is utilizing swap space heavily, it should be upgraded with additional memory to increase performance. Additionally, creating swap storage on its own dedicated disk is a good practice that is used to prevent degraded performance.*

`mkswap` is a Linux command. Similar commands exist on other platforms and are detailed in the following cross-reference table.

AIX	BSD	HP-UX	Linux	Solaris
mkps	swapctl	lvcreate	mkswap	swap

Swap command cross reference

Common usage examples:

`mkswap [DEVICE]`	Create swap space on the specified device
`mkswap -c [DEVICE]`	Check the device for bad blocks before formatting

swapon / swapoff

Purpose: Activate/deactivate swap space.

Usage syntax: swapon [OPTIONS] [DEVICE]

```
# swapon /dev/sdb1
```
Activating swap storage

The **swapon** command activates swap storage. The above example demonstrates activating a newly created swap space using **swapon**.

> | **Note** | *Newly created swap space does not become usable by the system until it is activated using the* **swapon** *command. Most systems have at least one swap space that is activated at boot by default. Additional swap devices created after installation must be added to the* /etc/fstab *file to be automatically activated at boot.* |

The **swapoff** command deactivates swap storage. The next example demonstrates using **swapoff** to deactivate the /dev/sdb1 swap device.

Usage syntax: swapoff [OPTIONS] [DEVICE]

```
# swapoff /dev/sdb1
```
Deactivating swap storage

Swap storage must be deactivated with the **swapoff** command before it can be changed or removed.

> | **Note** | *Solaris systems use the* **swap** *command in pace of* **swapon** *and* **swapoff***.* |

Common usage examples:

swapon -a	Enable all swap spaces
swapon [DEVICE]	Enable the specified swap space
swapon -s	Display swap usage by device
swapoff -a	Disable all active swap spaces
swapoff [DEVICE]	Disable the specified swap space

swapinfo

Purpose: Display swap space information.

Usage syntax: `swapinfo [OPTIONS]`

```
# swapinfo
             Kb        Kb       Kb PCT  START/       Kb
TYPE      AVAIL      USED     FREE USED LIMIT RESERVE PRI NAME
dev      524288         0   524288   0%     0       -     /dev/vg00/lvol2
reserve       -    111696  -111696
memory   389816    143784   246032  37%
```

Output of the swapinfo command on HP-UX

`swapinfo` displays details about active swap storage. The above example displays the output of the `swapinfo` command on an HP-UX system. It includes information about the size and location of swap storage and the amount of memory and swap utilization.

`swapinfo` is available on BSD and HP-UX systems. Other platforms use the commands listed in the cross-reference below to display information about swap utilization.

AIX	BSD	HP-UX	Linux	Solaris
lsps	swapinfo	swapinfo	free	swap

Swap command cross reference

Common usage examples:

swapinfo	Display swap space utilization on BSD and HP-UX systems

sync

Purpose: Flush file system buffers.

Usage syntax: `sync`

```
# sync
```

The `sync` command flushes the file system buffer. Unix, Linux, and BSD systems pool disk activity to increase performance. When this happens, pending write operations are buffered in memory and processed at an opportune time. The `sync` command forces the buffer to flush, which completes all pending write operations.

While the `sync` command is rarely used, it can be helpful in situations where the system must be rebooted in an abnormal manner, such as unplugging the system or pressing the reset button. Executing `sync` before powering off a system in this manner can help prevent file system corruption by ensuring all disk buffers are completely flushed.

Tip	*Executing the* `sync` *command twice is a common practice to ensure all file system buffers have been flushed. The can be done with one command by executing* `sync;sync` *on the command line.*

Common usage examples:

`sync`	Flush the file system buffer
`sync ; sync`	*Really* flush the file system buffer

Section 11:
Backup and Restore Commands

Overview

This section covers utilities used to backup and restore files. Creating a good backup is very important for recovering from system failure or natural disaster. Most systems have a number of built-in backup programs. These programs can create full, partial, and incremental backups and should be incorporated into your disaster recovery plan.

Commands covered in this section:

Command	Purpose
tar	Create/extract archive files.
dump	Create incremental backups.
restore	Restore files from dump archives.
dd	Create raw copies of data devices.
cpio	Create/extract cpio archives.
mt	Control tape devices.
mksysb	Create a backup image of an AIX system.

Glossary of terms used in this section:

Full Backup	A backup that includes all files on the local system.
Incremental Backup	A backup that includes only files that have changed since the last full backup.

tar

Purpose: Create/extract archive files.

Usage syntax: tar [OPTIONS] [OUTPUT] [INPUT]

```
# tar -cvf backup.tar /etc/*
/etc/acpi/
/etc/acpi/stopbtn.sh
/etc/acpi/videobtn.sh
/etc/acpi/ibm-wireless.sh
/etc/acpi/hibernate.sh
/etc/acpi/resume.d/
/etc/acpi/resume.d/15-video-post.sh
/etc/acpi/resume.d/62-ifup.sh
/etc/acpi/resume.d/10-thinkpad-standby-led.sh
...
```

Creating a backup archive of the /etc directory using the tar command

The **tar** command creates and extracts tar archives. It is the most commonly used utility for creating backups on Unix, Linux, and BSD systems. In the above example, the **-cvf** option is used to create a backup archive of the /etc directory called backup.tar.

In the next example, the **-xvf** option is used to extract the /etc/hosts file from the archive created in the first example.

```
# tar -xvf backup.tar etc/hosts
etc/hosts
```

Extracting files from a tar archive

Note	*The default operation of the* **tar** *command strips the leading* / *from the file path. This means that files restored from* **tar** *archives will be placed in a location relative to the current directory. The* **-P** *option can be specified to override this behavior.*

Common usage examples:

tar -cvf [FILE] [ITEM]	Backup the specified item(s)
tar -czvf [FILE] [ITEM]	Compress the archive to save space
tar -xvf [FILE] [ITEM]	Restore the specified item(s)
tar -tf [FILE]	List all files in the specified archive

dump

Purpose: Create incremental backups.

Usage syntax: `dump [OPTIONS] [OUTPUT] [INPUT]`

```
# dump -0 -uf backup.dump /
```
Creating a full backup using the dump command

`dump` is an archive utility that creates incremental backups. In the above example, the `-0` option indicates a full backup of the `/` file system to a file called `backup.dump`.

Subsequent incremental backups are specified as `-1`, `-2`, `-3`, etc. The subsequent backups will only archive files that have changed since the last full backup. This can save time and storage space when creating backups, but it will take longer to restore since the incremental backups must be restored in layers.

> **Note**
>
> *Information about backed up files is stored in a file called* `dumpdates`. *On Unix systems, this file is usually found in* `/etc/dumpdates`. *Linux systems store this information in* `/var/lib/dumpdates`.

Common usage examples:

`dump -0 -uf [OUTPUT] [INPUT]`	Create a full backup
`dump -[NUM] -uf [OUTPUT] [INPUT]`	Create an incremental backup

restore

Purpose: Restore files from dump archives.

Usage syntax: `restore [OPTIONS] [FILE]`

```
# restore -if backup.dump
restore > pwd
/
restore > cd etc
restore > add hosts
restore > extract
...
```

Restoring files from a dump archive

The **restore** command restores files from archives created with the **dump** command. The above example demonstrates starting the interactive **restore** shell to extract files from a **dump** archive.

The following table describes the basic **restore** shell commands.

Command	Function
ls [PATH]	List the contents of the current or specified directory
cd [PATH]	Navigate the dump archive
pwd	Display the current working directory
add [PATH]	Add the current directory (or specified item) to the restore list
delete [PATH]	Delete the current directory (or specified item) from the restore list
extract	Extract all files on the restore list
help	Display the help menu
quit	Exit the restore shell

Restore shell commands

Common usage examples:

restore -if [FILE]	Open the specified archive in the restore shell
restore -rf [FILE]	Restore an entire file system from a dump archive
restore -tf [FILE]	List all items in the specified dump archive

dd

Purpose: Create raw copies of data devices.

Usage syntax: `dd if=[SOURCE] of=[TARGET] [OPTIONS]`

```
# dd if=/dev/sdb of=/dev/sdc
```
Creating a copy of a disk using the dd command

The `dd` command performs raw (bit for bit) copies of data devices. The `if` parameter specifies the input file or device to be read. The `of` parameter specifies the output location. In the above example, the entire hard drive `/dev/sdb` is copied to `/dev/sdc`.

`dd` can also be used to create image files of a disk. The next example demonstrates using `dd` to create an ISO image file from a CD-ROM.

```
# dd if=/dev/cdrom of=/tmp/image.iso
```
Converting a CD-ROM into an ISO file using the dd command

Warning	*The* `dd` *command is often referred to as the "data destroyer" because it can be very destructive if used incorrectly. Always use caution when experimenting with* `dd`.

Common usage examples:

`dd if=[SOURCE] of=[TARGET]` | Create a raw copy of the specified device

207

cpio

Purpose: Create or extract cpio archives.

Usage syntax: `[INPUT] | cpio [OPTIONS] > [OUTPUT]`

```
# cd /etc
# ls | cpio -ov > /tmp/backup.cpio
adduser.conf
adjtime
aliases
alternatives
...
```
Creating a backup with the cpio command

The `cpio` utility creates simple backups. In the above example, the `-ov` option creates a `cpio` backup of the `/etc` directory.

The next example demonstrates restoring files from the `backup.cpio` archive using the `-idv` option.

```
# cd /etc
# cpio -idv < /tmp/backup.cpio
adduser.conf
adjtime
aliases
alternatives
...
```
Extracting files from a cpio archive

Note	`cpio` is a legacy program that is rarely used for backup on modern systems. Use `tar` and `dump` in place of `cpio` as they offer a more complete and user-friendly backup solution.

Common usage examples:

`ls	cpio -ov > backup.cpio`	Backup the specified item(s)
`cpio -idv < backup.cpio`	Restore the specified item(s)
`cpio --list < backup.cpio`	List all items in the specified archive

mt

Purpose: Control tape devices.

Usage syntax: `mt -f [DEVICE] [OPERATION]`

```
# mt -f /dev/rmt0 rewind
```

Rewinding a tape using the mt command

The `mt` command controls removable tape devices. It can be used to display the status of the drive and manage its removable media. The example above demonstrates using the `mt` command to rewind the tape in the `/dev/rmt0` drive.

The following table lists the most common operations used with the `mt` utility.

Operation	Function
rewind	Rewind the tape device
retension	Retension the tape
erase	Erase the tape
status	Display the tape device status
offline	Rewind and eject the tape

Common mt operations

Common usage examples:

`mt -f [DEVICE] [OPERATION]` | Execute the specified operation on a tape drive

mksysb

Purpose: Create a backup image of an AIX system.

Usage syntax: mksysb [OPTIONS] [DEVICE/FILE]

```
# mksysb -i /dev/rmt0

Creating information file (/image.data) for rootvg.

Creating list of files to back up.

Backing up 64981 files.............................
51767 of 64981 files (79%)..

64981 of 64981 files (100%)
0512-038 mksysb: Backup Completed Successfully.
```

Creating a mksysb backup on AIX

The **mksysb** command creates a backup image of an AIX system. This image can be used to restore the base operating system in the event of system failure.

In the above example a **mksysb** system image is written to the /dev/rmt0 tape device.

> **Note**
>
> **mksysb** *is not a substitute for a traditional backup as is does not include files outside of the base operating system. Databases, 3rd party software, etc. are not backed up in a* **mksysb** *image. These files should be backed up separately using another method (such as the* **tar** *command.)*

Common usage examples:

mksysb -i [DEVICE/FILE] | Create a system image backup

Section 12:
Monitoring and Troubleshooting

Overview

This section covers commands used to monitor and troubleshoot Unix, Linux, and BSD systems. These commands can be used to diagnose problems or resolve performance problems.

Commands covered in this section:

Command	Purpose
top	Monitor system performance and running processes.
htop	Advanced system monitor for Linux.
topas	Performance monitor for AIX systems.
iotop	Monitor disk input and output operations.
mpstat	Display processor utilization information.
vmstat	Display virtual memory usage information.
iostat	Display I/O utilization statistics.
dstat	Monitor CPU, disk, network, and swap utilization.
nfsstat	Display NFS statistics.
free	Display system memory and swap space usage information.
df	Display file system usage information.
du	Display disk usage.
uname	Display information about the operating system.
uptime	Display how long the system has been online.
dmesg	Display kernel log messages.
errpt	Display system error messages on AIX systems.
strace	Trace system calls and signals.
ltrace	Trace library calls.
lsmod	Display Linux kernel module information.
insmod rmmod	Install/remove kernel modules.
modinfo	Display information about Linux kernel modules.

(Continued...)

Command	Purpose
`sysctl`	Display and edit kernel parameters on Linux and BSD systems.

Glossary of terms used in this section:

I/O	(Input/Output) The process of reading or writing to a disk drive.
Kernel Module	An extension to the kernel that provides a driver, feature, or service.
Library	A collection of subroutines used by applications.
Load Average	The average of system load over a period of time.
System Call	The process of a program requesting access to system resources such as kernel facilities or system hardware.
Trace	The process of monitoring internal functions of a program such as system calls and library calls.
Virtual Memory	A logical combination of physical memory and swap storage.

top

Purpose: Monitor system performance and running processes.

Usage syntax: `top [OPTIONS]`

```
$ top
top - 18:56:55 up 21 min,  2 users,  load average: 0.22, 0.35, 0.31
Tasks: 140 total,   2 running, 138 sleeping,   0 stopped,   0 zombie
Cpu(s): 9.0%us, 2.0%sy, 0.1%ni, 85.1%id, 3.5%wa, 0.1%hi, 0.2%si, 0.0%st
Mem:   3988516k total,  1089196k used,  2899320k free,   35832k buffers
Swap:  3951948k total,       0k used,  3951948k free,  664684k cached
```

PID	USER	PR	NI	VIRT	RES	SHR	S	%CPU	%MEM	TIME+	COMMAND
5297	nick	20	0	19112	1224	892	R	4	0.0	0:00.02	top
1	root	20	0	4100	920	632	S	0	0.0	0:01.16	init
2	root	15	-5	0	0	0	S	0	0.0	0:00.00	kthreadd
3	root	RT	-5	0	0	0	S	0	0.0	0:00.00	migration/0
4	root	15	-5	0	0	0	S	0	0.0	0:00.82	ksoftirqd/0
5	root	RT	-5	0	0	0	S	0	0.0	0:00.00	watchdog/0
6	root	RT	-5	0	0	0	S	0	0.0	0:00.00	migration/1
7	root	15	-5	0	0	0	S	0	0.0	0:00.06	ksoftirqd/1
8	root	RT	-5	0	0	0	S	0	0.0	0:00.00	watchdog/1
9	root	15	-5	0	0	0	S	0	0.0	0:00.01	events/0
10	root	15	-5	0	0	0	S	0	0.0	0:00.04	events/1
11	root	15	-5	0	0	0	S	0	0.0	0:00.00	khelper

Monitoring system activity with the top command

`top` is a process and performance monitor for Unix, Linux, and BSD systems. The first few lines of `top` output displays information about processor, memory, and swap utilization. The remaining portion of the screen is used to display information about running processes. The process listing updates every few seconds to display the most resource-intensive processes.

> **Tip**
>
> *There are several interactive commands that can be used to control the output of the `top` command. Press the `?` key within `top` for a complete listing of these commands.*

Common usage examples:

`top`	Monitor system performance and processes
`top -u [USER]`	Only display processes owned by the specified user
`top -d [SECONDS]`	Update at the specified interval (in seconds)
`top -i`	Do not display idle processes

htop

Purpose: Advanced system monitor for Linux.

Usage syntax: `htop`

```
CPU[                           3.8%]    Tasks: 26 total, 1 running
Mem[| ||||||||            33/1002MB]    Load average: 0.00 0.00 0.01
Swp[                      0/400MB]      Uptime: 00:41:30

  PID USER      PRI  NI  VIRT   RES   SHR S CPU% MEM%  TIME+   Command
 4112 nmarsh     20   0  2500  1232   960 R  3.0  0.1  0:01.53 htop
    1 root       20   0  2520  1400  1096 S  0.0  0.1  0:01.48 /sbin/init
  292 root       20   0  2148   764   568 S  0.0  0.1  0:00.08 upstart-udev-bridg
  304 root       16  -4  2316   860   384 S  0.0  0.1  0:00.28 udevd --daemon
  490 root       20   0  1848   544   448 S  0.0  0.1  0:00.59 dd bs=1 if=/proc/k
  497 syslog     20   0 33300  1304   976 S  0.0  0.1  0:00.02 rsyslogd -c4
  507 syslog     20   0 33300  1304   976 S  0.0  0.1  0:00.00 rsyslogd -c4
  508 syslog     20   0 33300  1304   976 S  0.0  0.1  0:00.00 rsyslogd -c4
 4071 syslog     20   0 33300  1304   976 S  0.0  0.1  0:00.00 rsyslogd -c4
  626 root       20   0  2140   312   184 S  0.0  0.0  0:00.00 dhclient3 -e IF_ME
  657 root       20   0  1700   548   464 S  0.0  0.1  0:00.00 /sbin/getty -8 384
  659 root       20   0  1700   540   464 S  0.0  0.1  0:00.00 /sbin/getty -8 384
  663 root       20   0  1700   544   464 S  0.0  0.1  0:00.00 /sbin/getty -8 384
  664 root       20   0  1700   544   464 S  0.0  0.1  0:00.00 /sbin/getty -8 384
  667 root       20   0  1700   544   464 S  0.0  0.1  0:00.00 /sbin/getty -8 384
  675 daemon     20   0  1960   420   292 S  0.0  0.0  0:00.00 atd
  676 root       20   0  2088   860   684 S  0.0  0.1  0:00.08 cron
F1Help  F2Setup  F3Search F4Invert F5Tree  F6SortBy F7Nice - F8Nice + F9Kill  F10Quit
```

Monitoring system activity with htop

`htop` is an alternative system monitor for Linux that is similar to the previously discussed `top` command. The example above displays a screenshot of the `htop` interface. It features color output and uses a graphical scale to visualize processor, memory, and swap utilization.

> **Tip**
> *Similar to* `top`, `htop` *supports interactive commands. Press the* **F1** *key within* `htop` *for a complete listing of interactive options.*

Common usage examples:

`htop`	Run the top monitor with default settings
`htop -u [USER]`	Only display processes from the specified user

topas

Purpose: Performance monitor for AIX systems.

Usage syntax: `topas [OPTIONS]`

```
# topas
Topas Monitor for host:     localhost             EVENTS/QUEUES    FILE/TTY
Sat May 15 16:16:19 2010    Interval:  2          Cswitch     63   Readch     1228
                                                  Syscall     74   Writech     176
CPU   User%  Kern%  Wait%  Idle%                  Reads        2   Rawin         0
ALL    0.0    0.0    0.0   100.0                  Writes       3   Ttyout     1226
                                                  Forks        0   Igets         0
Network  KBPS  I-Pack  O-Pack  KB-In  KB-Out      Execs        0   Namei         4
Total     1.4    2.5     2.5     0.1    1.3       Runqueue   0.0   Dirblk        0
                                                  Waitqueue  0.0
Disk   Busy%    KBPS    TPS  KB-Read  KB-Writ                      MEMORY
Total   0.0     0.0     0.0    0.0      0.0       PAGING           Real,MB    2048
                                                  Faults       0   % Comp       36
FileSystem       KBPS    TPS  KB-Read  KB-Writ    Steals       0   % Noncomp     7
Total             1.2    1.5    1.2      0.0       PgspIn       0   % Client      7
                                                  PgspOut      0
Name           PID  CPU%  PgSp  Owner             PageIn       0   PAGING SPACE
topas       221296   0.1   1.3  root              PageOut      0   Size,MB     512
java        286878   0.0  49.4  pconsole          Sios         0   % Used        1
telnetd     307338   0.0   0.7  root                               % Free       99
netm         40980   0.0   0.1  root                           Press: "h"-help
cimserve    319686   0.0  30.5  root                                   "q"-quit
```

Screenshot of the topas monitor for AIX

`topas` is the performance monitor for AIX systems. Executing `topas` with no options shows an overview of all areas of system utilization, as shown in the above example.

`topas` also has several options to monitor specific aspects of the system. For example, the `-D` option displays disk utilization information for each disk on the system as shown in the next example.

```
# topas -D
Topas Monitor for host:    localhost   Interval:   2    Sat May 15 16:43:32 2010
=============================================================================
Disk    Busy%  KBPS    TPS    KB-R   ART   MRT   KB-W   AWT   MWT   AQW   AQD
hdisk1   0.0   0.0     0.0    0.0    0.0   0.0   0.0    0.0   0.0   0.0   0.0
hdisk0   0.0   2.7K   701.0   2.7K   1.0  42.1   0.0    0.0   0.0   0.0   0.0
```

Screenshot of the topas monitor for AIX

Common usage examples:

topas	Display the topas monitor
topas -D	Monitor disk activity
topas -P	Monitor processes
topas -V	Monitor volume group activity
topas -F	Monitor file system activity
topas -E	Monitor ethernet activity

iotop

Purpose: Monitor disk input and output operations.

Usage syntax: `iotop [OPTIONS]`

```
$ iotop
Total DISK READ: 52.68 M/s | Total DISK WRITE: 0.00 B/s
  TID  PRIO  USER   DISK READ   DISK WRITE   SWAPIN       IO>     COMMAND
 4310 be/4  root     9.33 M/s    0.00 B/s   0.00 %     0.00 % hdparm -Tt
 4311 be/4  root     4.84 M/s    0.00 B/s   0.00 %     0.00 % hdparm -Tt
 4312 be/4  root     9.46 M/s    0.00 B/s   0.00 %     0.00 % hdparm -Tt
 4313 be/4  root    13.68 M/s    0.00 B/s   0.00 %     0.00 % hdparm
    1 be/4  root     0.00 B/s    0.00 B/s   0.00 %     0.00 % init
    2 be/3  root     0.00 B/s    0.00 B/s   0.00 %     0.00 % [kthreadd]
    3 rt/3  root     0.00 B/s    0.00 B/s   0.00 %     0.00 % [migration/0]
    4 be/3  root     0.00 B/s    0.00 B/s   0.00 %     0.00 % [ksoftirqd/0]
    5 rt/3  root     0.00 B/s    0.00 B/s   0.00 %     0.00 % [watchdog/0]
    6 be/3  root     0.00 B/s    0.00 B/s   0.00 %     0.00 % [events/0]
    7 be/3  root     0.00 B/s    0.00 B/s   0.00 %     0.00 % [cpuset]
    8 be/3  root     0.00 B/s    0.00 B/s   0.00 %     0.00 % [khelper]
    9 be/3  root     0.00 B/s    0.00 B/s   0.00 %     0.00 % [netns]
   10 be/3  root     0.00 B/s    0.00 B/s   0.00 %     0.00 % [async/mgr]
   11 be/3  root     0.00 B/s    0.00 B/s   0.00 %     0.00 % [kintegrityd/0]
   12 be/3  root     0.00 B/s    0.00 B/s   0.00 %     0.00 % [kblockd/0]
   13 be/3  root     0.00 B/s    0.00 B/s   0.00 %     0.00 % [kacpid]
   14 be/3  root     0.00 B/s    0.00 B/s   0.00 %     0.00 % [kacpi_notify]
   15 be/3  root     0.00 B/s    0.00 B/s   0.00 %     0.00 % [kacpi_hotplug]
   16 be/3  root     0.00 B/s    0.00 B/s   0.00 %     0.00 % [ata/0]
   17 be/3  root     0.00 B/s    0.00 B/s   0.00 %     0.00 % [ata_aux]
```

Monitoring disk utilization using iotop

`iotop` is a utility for monitoring disk I/O operations on Linux systems. It can be useful for monitoring disk performance and tracking down resource intensive applications. The example above displays the default `iotop` interface.

> **Tip** *Press the **Q** key to exit the `iotop` utility.*

Common usage examples:

`iotop`	Monitor system I/O statistics
`iotop -o`	Only display processes performing I/O
`iotop -u [USER]`	Only display I/O activity from the specified user
`iotop -d [SECONDS]`	Update at the specified interval (in seconds)

mpstat

Purpose: Display processor utilization information.

Usage syntax: `mpstat [OPTIONS] [DELAY] [COUNT]`

```
$ mpstat 2 10
Linux 2.6.24-19-server (vmware-02)      05/03/2010

10:46:53 AM  CPU  %user  %nice  %sys  %iowait  %irq  %soft  %steal  %idle  intr/s
10:46:55 AM  all  0.00   0.00   2.22   0.00     0.00  0.00   0.00    97.78   82.50
10:46:57 AM  all  0.62   0.00   2.49   0.00     0.00  0.00   0.00    96.89  126.50
10:46:59 AM  all  0.12   0.00   2.21   0.00     0.00  0.12   0.00    97.54   84.00
10:47:01 AM  all  0.25   0.00   5.29   0.62     0.12  0.00   0.00    93.73  403.00
10:47:03 AM  all  0.00   0.00   2.55   0.00     0.00  0.00   0.00    97.45  106.50
10:47:05 AM  all  0.25   0.00   2.84   0.00     0.00  0.00   0.00    96.91  101.50
10:47:07 AM  all  0.00   0.00   3.28   0.00     0.00  0.00   0.00    96.72  118.00
10:47:09 AM  all  0.24   0.00   3.40   0.00     0.00  0.00   0.00    96.36  126.00
10:47:11 AM  all  0.00   0.00   3.91   0.00     0.00  0.00   0.00    96.09   97.50
10:47:13 AM  all  0.00   0.00   3.27   0.00     0.12  0.00   0.00    96.61  107.00
Average:     all  0.15   0.00   3.15   0.06     0.02  0.01   0.00    96.61  135.25
```

Output of the mpstat command

`mpstat` displays processor utilization information on Linux systems. In the above example, executing `mpstat 2 10` instructs the program to display results in two second intervals and exit after displaying 10 lines. If the delay and count options are omitted `mpstat` will display one line of results and then terminate.

Common usage examples:

`mpstat`	Display processor utilization once and exit
`mpstat [DELAY]`	Update display at the specified interval
`mpstat [DELAY] [COUNT]`	End monitoring after reaching the specified count

vmstat

Purpose: Display virtual memory usage information.

Usage syntax: vmstat [OPTIONS] [DELAY] [COUNT]

```
# vmstat 2 10
procs -----------memory---------- ---swap-- -----io---- -system-- ----cpu----
 r  b   swpd   free   buff  cache   si   so    bi    bo   in   cs us sy id wa
 0  0     88  79260 149184 7400704    0    0     0    93    1    4  0  2 97  0
 0  1     88  78996 149184 7400704    0    0     0     2  119 2933  0  4 90  6
 2  0     88  78996 149184 7400704    0    0     0    12  115 3083  0  3 94  3
 0  0     88  78872 149184 7400704    0    0     0  1828  259 3275  0  3 97  0
 0  0     88  78872 149184 7400704    0    0     0    62  145 3031  0  4 96  0
 0  0     88  78748 149184 7400704    0    0     0     0  114 2965  0  2 98  0
 0  0     88  78452 149184 7400704    0    0     0   498  150 3170  0  3 97  0
 0  0     88  78004 149184 7400704    0    0     0     0  114 3073  0  3 97  0
 0  0     88  77632 149184 7400704    0    0     0   198  306 4659  0  5 95  0
 0  0     88  77260 149184 7400708    0    0     0    52  130 2864  0  3 97  0
```

Displaying memory utilization using the vmstat command

The **vmstat** command displays virtual memory statistics. In the above example, executing **vmstat 2 10** instructs the program to display results in two second intervals and exit after displaying 10 lines. If the delay and count parameters are omitted, **vmstat** will display one line of results and then terminate.

> **Tip**
>
> The **-Sm** option can be used with the **vmstat** command on some systems to display the memory totals in megabytes instead of kilobytes.

Common usage examples:

vmstat	Display memory utilization once and exit
vmstat [DELAY]	Update results at the specified interval
vmstat [DELAY] [COUNT]	End after reaching the specified count
vmstat -s	Display a table of memory statistics
vmstat -Sm	Display utilization in megabytes

iostat

Purpose: Display I/O utilization statistics.

Usage syntax: `iostat [OPTIONS] [DELAY] [COUNT]`

```
# iostat -d 2 5
Linux 2.6.24-19-server (vmware-02)      05/03/2010

Device:           tps    Blk_read/s   Blk_wrtn/s   Blk_read   Blk_wrtn
sda             56.65          3.44       756.95    9462264 2080033488

Device:           tps    Blk_read/s   Blk_wrtn/s   Blk_read   Blk_wrtn
sda              3.50          0.00        64.00          0        128

Device:           tps    Blk_read/s   Blk_wrtn/s   Blk_read   Blk_wrtn
sda              6.97          0.00        59.70          0        120

Device:           tps    Blk_read/s   Blk_wrtn/s   Blk_read   Blk_wrtn
sda              0.00          0.00         0.00          0          0

Device:           tps    Blk_read/s   Blk_wrtn/s   Blk_read   Blk_wrtn
sda             61.50          0.00       524.00          0       1048
```

Displaying I/O utilization using the iostat command

The `iostat` command displays I/O utilization statistics for disk drives and network file systems. It is helpful in monitoring disk drives as they can be a significant bottleneck in system performance. In the above example, five lines of I/O statistics are displayed. The first line displays the statistics since the system was last booted. Subsequent lines display the totals since the previous line was printed.

Common usage examples:

`iostat`	Display I/O utilization once and exit
`iostat [DELAY]`	Update I/O utilization at the specified interval
`iostat [DELAY] [COUNT]`	End after reaching the specified count
`iostat -k`	Display statistics in kilobytes per second
`iostat -m`	Display statistics in megabytes per second
`iostat -d`	Only display I/O devices
`iostat -p`	Display each partition individually
`iostat -n`	Display NFS I/O utilization

dstat

Purpose: Monitor CPU, disk, network, and swap utilization.

Usage syntax: `dstat [OPTIONS] [DELAY] [COUNT]`

```
$ dstat 2 10
----total-cpu-usage---- -dsk/total- -net/total- ---paging-- ---system--
usr sys idl wai hiq siq| read  writ| recv  send|  in   out | int   csw
  0   2  97   0   0   0|1763B 379k|   0     0 |   0     0 | 131  2611
  0   9  91   0   0   0|   0     0 | 346k  99k|   0     0 | 482  4748
  0   3  97   0   0   0|   0   410k| 141k  16k|   0     0 | 125  3189
  0   3  97   0   0   0|   0     0 |  55k 9090B|   0     0 | 114  3054
  0   3  96   0   0   0|   0     0 |  55k  9.9k|   0     0 | 100  2723
  0   4  96   0   0   0| 376k  63k|  63k  11k|   0     0 | 115  2904
  0   3  96   0   0   0|   0     0 |  55k  9.8k|   0     0 | 127  3221
  0   2  98   0   0   0| 182k  64k|  64k  13k|   0     0 | 135  3067
  0   2  97   0   0   0|   0     0 |  55k  10k|   0     0 | 115  2925
  0   4  96   0   0   0|   0     0 |  54k 9832B|   0     0 | 118  3129
  0  13  87   0   0   0|  94k  37k|  37k  11k|   0     0 | 548  4950
```

Monitoring system performance using the dstat command

dstat is an all-in-one performance monitoring utility for Linux systems. The above example demonstrates the default output of **dstat** which displays CPU, disk, network, and swap utilization in a single and easy-to-read display.

> **Tip**
>
> **dstat** *output can be custom-tailored to your needs using a number of command line options. See* **man dstat** *for more information.*

Common usage examples:

`dstat`	Monitor system utilization
`dstat [DELAY]`	Update results at the specified interval
`dstat [DELAY] [COUNT]`	End monitoring after reaching the specified count

nfsstat

Purpose: Display NFS statistics.

Usage syntax: `nfsstat [OPTIONS]`

```
# nfsstat
Server rpc stats:
calls        badcalls  badauth      badclnt      xdrcall
1            0         0            0            0

Server nfs v3:
null         getattr     setattr       lookup       access        readlink
1       100% 0        0% 0          0% 0          0% 0          0% 0          0%
read         write       create        mkdir        symlink       mknod
0         0% 0        0% 0          0% 0          0% 0          0% 0          0%
remove       rmdir       rename        link         readdir       readdirplus
0         0% 0        0% 0          0% 0          0% 0          0% 0          0%
fsstat       fsinfo      pathconf      commit
0         0% 0        0% 0          0% 0          0%

Client rpc stats:
calls        retrans   authrefrsh
2924         0         0

Client nfs v3:
null         getattr     setattr       lookup       access        readlink
0         0% 2761    94% 0          0% 2          0% 87         2% 0          0%
read         write       create        mkdir        symlink       mknod
1         0% 0        0% 0          0% 3          0% 0          0% 0          0%
remove       rmdir       rename        link         readdir       readdirplus
0         0% 0        0% 0          0% 0          0% 0          0% 66         2%
fsstat       fsinfo      pathconf      commit
0         0% 2        0% 1          0% 0          0%
```
Displaying NFS statistics

`nfsstat` displays NFS utilization statistics. This can be helpful for monitoring performance of NFS services. The above example shows various utilization indicators for the NFS client and server running on the local system

Common usage examples:

`nfsstat`	Display all NFS statistics
`nfsstat -s`	Display server statistics only
`nfsstat -c`	Display client statistics only

free

Purpose: Display system memory and swap space usage information.

Usage syntax: `free [OPTIONS]`

```
$ free
              total       used       free     shared    buffers     cached
Mem:        8186412    8136752      49660          0     181960    7352700
-/+ buffers/cache:      602092    7584320
Swap:      23695832         88   23695744
```

Displaying memory and swap space utilization using the free command

`free` displays memory and swap space utilization on Linux systems. The default output of the `free` command displays totals in kilobytes, as displayed in the above example. The next example demonstrates using the `-m` option which produces a more "human friendly" output in megabytes.

```
$ free -m
              total       used       free     shared    buffers     cached
Mem:           7994       7946         48          0        177       7180
-/+ buffers/cache:         588       7406
Swap:         23140          0      23140
```

Displaying memory and swap space utilization in "human friendly" format

Common usage examples:

`free`	Display memory usage in kilobytes
`free -m`	Display memory usage in megabytes
`free -g`	Display memory usage in gigabytes

df

Purpose: Display file system usage information.

Usage syntax: df [OPTIONS]

```
$ df -h
Filesystem              Size  Used  Avail  Use%  Mounted on
/dev/sda6               143G  9.1G   127G   7%   /
/dev/sdb1               466G  426G    41G  92%   /media/Seagate
tmpfs                   2.0G     0   2.0G   0%   /lib/init/rw
varrun                  2.0G  104K   2.0G   1%   /var/run
varlock                 2.0G     0   2.0G   0%   /var/lock
udev                    2.0G  172K   2.0G   1%   /dev
tmpfs                   2.0G  508K   2.0G   1%   /dev/shm
lrm                     2.0G  2.7M   1.9G   1%   /lib/modules/2.6.28-11
```

Typical output of the df command

The **df** command displays file system usage information on Unix, Linux, and BSD systems. The resulting output displays the size, used space, and available space for each file system.

On some systems, **df** will also display information about pseudo file systems. These file systems typically do not contain real files and exist only in memory to provide access to kernel facilities. In the above example, the first two lines are actual file systems and the remaining entries are pseudo file systems.

> **Tip**
>
> Some systems may support the use of the −h parameter as shown in the above example. This option displays "human readable" output in kilobytes, megabytes, and gigabytes as opposed to the default unit of measure (which is usually 1k or 512k blocks). See **man df** to verify the unit of measure used by default on your local system.

Common usage examples:

df	Display file system usage information
df -h	Display sizes in human readable format (i.e., megabytes and gigabytes)

du

Purpose: Display disk usage.

Usage syntax: du [OPTIONS] [DIRECTORY/FILE]

```
$ du -hs /usr
523M    /usr
```

Using the du command to display the size of a directory

The **du** command displays information about disk usage. It can display the size of a specific directory or group of files. The above example demonstrates using the **du** command to display the size of the /usr directory. The **-hs** option instructs **du** to show summarized results in "human readable" form. Omitting the **-s** option will recursively display the size of each file under /usr, as demonstrated below.

```
$ du -h /usr/
4.0K    /usr/local/etc
1.4M    /usr/local/bin
4.0K    /usr/local/games
4.0K    /usr/local/src
4.0K    /usr/local/sbin
224K    /usr/local/share/man/man1
228K    /usr/local/share/man
```

Displaying the size of files using the du command

Some systems may not support the **-h** parameter. In this case, the **du** command will display file sizes in blocks rather than a "human readable" unit of measure, as shown in the next example.

```
$ du -s /usr
534884  /usr
```

Output of the du command on older Unix systems

Common usage examples:

du -hs	Display the size of the current directory
du -hs [DIRECTORY]	Display the size of the specified directory
du -h [DIRECTORY]	Display the size of each file in the specified directory

uname

Purpose: Display information about the operating system.

Usage syntax: `uname [OPTIONS]`

```
# uname -a
Linux mylaptop 2.6.28-11-generic x86_64 GNU/Linux
```
Output of the uname command on Linux systems

uname displays information and the hardware and software versions installed on the system. This includes information such as processor type, kernel version, and hardware platform for the local system.

The above example displays uname output on a Linux system. The next example displays the output on an HP-UX system.

```
# uname -a
HP-UX server1 B.10.20 C 9000/861 32-user license
```
Output of the uname command on HP-UX systems

The output of the uname varies across platforms. The table below describes the typical information displayed when executing uname -a.

Platform	Hostname	Version	Hardware	Other
Linux	mylaptop	2.6.28-11-generic	x86_64	GNU/Linux
HP-UX	server1	B.10.20 C	9000/861	32-user license

Common usage examples:

uname -a	Display all information
uname -r	Display the kernel version number

uptime

Purpose: Display how long the system has been online.

Usage syntax: `uptime`

```
$ uptime
 19:15:55 up 2 days 40 min,  2 users,   load average: 0.13, 1.15, 1.24
```
Output of the uptime command

The `uptime` command displays how long a system has been online since the last shutdown or restart. It also displays the number of users currently logged into the system and the CPU load average.

The load average information displays three numeric fields. These represent three samples of system load taken over the last 1, 5, and 15 minutes. The lower the number, the lower the system load is. For example, on a single CPU system, a .13 load average correlates to a 13% load. A 1.15 load average would be a 115% load meaning that the system is 15% overloaded because processes have to wait 15% of the time for system resources (such as CPU and disk I/O).

Note	*The load average is displayed for informational purposes only. It is not meant to be used as an accurate performance gauge, as it can be affected by various factors.*

Common usage examples:

`uptime`	Display system uptime and load average information

dmesg

Purpose: Display kernel log messages.

Usage syntax: dmesg [OPTIONS]

```
# dmesg | less
[0.000000] Initializing cgroup subsys cpuset
[0.000000] Initializing cgroup subsys cpu
[0.000000] Linux version 2.6.24-27-server (buildd@palmer) (gcc version
4.2.4 (Ubuntu 4.2.4-1ubuntu3)) #1 SMP Fri Mar 12 01:45:06 UTC 2010
(Ubuntu 2.6.24-27.68-server)
[0.000000] BIOS-provided physical RAM map:
[0.000000]  BIOS-e820: 0000000000000000 - 000000000009f800 (usable)
[0.000000]  BIOS-e820: 000000000009f800 - 00000000000a0000 (reserved)
[0.000000]  BIOS-e820: 00000000000ca000 - 00000000000cc000 (reserved)
[0.000000]  BIOS-e820: 00000000000dc000 - 0000000000100000 (reserved)
. . .
```

Displaying kernel messages using dmesg

The **dmesg** command displays the kernel message log. This is the first place you should check when troubleshooting a problem. Executing **dmesg** displays all messages in the kernel log buffer, as demonstrated in the above example.

dmesg output can be very lengthy. Using **grep** with the **demsg** command is helpful to search for a specific message. The next example demonstrates filtering **dmesg** using **grep** to search for the word *fail*.

```
$ demsg | grep fail
[39176.231722] usb-storage: probe of 2-2:1.0 failed with error -5
[41421.627352] PM: Device 2-2 failed to resume: error -19
[41429.152942] usb-storage: probe of 2-3:1.0 failed with error -5
[46938.994016] usb-storage: probe of 2-3:1.0 failed with error -5
[49869.891317] usb-storage: probe of 2-3:1.0 failed with error -5
[57103.036672] PM: Device 2-3 failed to resume: error -19
. . .
```

Searching dmesg output for an error message

> **Tip** *Kernel messages are typically stored in the* /var/log/dmesg *file.*

Common usage examples:

dmesg	Display the kernel log
dmesg -c	Clear all kernel log messages

errpt

Purpose: Display system error messages on AIX systems.

Usage syntax: `errpt [OPTIONS]`

```
# errpt
IDENTIFIER TIMESTAMP  T C RESOURCE_NAME  DESCRIPTION
A6DF45AA   0515143110 I O RMCdaemon      The daemon is started.
2BFA76F6   0515142910 T S SYSPROC        SYSTEM SHUTDOWN BY USER
9DBCFDEE   0515143010 T O errdemon       ERROR LOGGING TURNED ON
67145A39   0510232410 U S SYSDUMP        SYSTEM DUMP
BE0A03E5   0510232410 P H sysplanar0     ENVIRONMENTAL PROBLEM
F48137AC   0510232410 U O minidump       COMPRESSED MINIMAL DUMP
BFE4C025   0510231210 P H sysplanar0     UNDETERMINED ERROR
...
```

Example output of the errpt command

errpt displays the error log on IBM AIX systems. It can be helpful when troubleshooting problems with system hardware and software. Executing the errpt command displays a short list of logged errors as shown in the above example. The -a option can be used with errpt to display detailed information about each error, as shown in the next example.

```
# errpt -a
---------------------------------------------------------------------
LABEL:            EPOW_SUS_CHRP
IDENTIFIER:       BE0A03E5

Date/Time:        Sat May 15 14:29:54 CDT 2010
Sequence Number:  47
Machine Id:       0008A41D4C00
Node Id:          localhost
Class:            H
Type:             PERM
WPAR:             Global
Resource Name:    sysplanar0
...
```

Output of the errpt -a command

Tip	*To clear the AIX error log, execute* `errclear` 0 *as the root user.*

Common usage examples:

`errpt`	Display a summary of system errors
`errpt -a`	Display detailed information for all errors
`errpt -aj [IDENTIFIER]`	Display detailed information for a specific error

strace

Purpose: Trace system calls and signals.

Usage syntax: `strace [OPTIONS] [PROGRAM]`

```
$ strace ls
open("/usr/lib/locale/en_US.utf8/LC_NAME", O_RDONLY) = 3
fstat64(3, {st_mode=S_IFREG|0644, st_size=77, ...}) = 0
mmap2(NULL, 77, PROT_READ, MAP_PRIVATE, 3, 0) = 0xb75f8000
close(3)                                  = 0
open("/usr/lib/locale/en_US.UTF-8/LC_PAPER", O_RDONLY) = -1 ENOENT (No
such file or directory)
open("/usr/lib/locale/en_US.utf8/LC_PAPER", O_RDONLY) = 3
fstat64(3, {st_mode=S_IFREG|0644, st_size=34, ...}) = 0
mmap2(NULL, 34, PROT_READ, MAP_PRIVATE, 3, 0) = 0xb75f7000
close(3)                                  = 0
open("/usr/lib/locale/en_US.UTF-8/LC_MESSAGES", O_RDONLY) = -1 ENOENT
(No such file or directory)
open("/usr/lib/locale/en_US.utf8/LC_MESSAGES", O_RDONLY) = 3
fstat64(3, {st_mode=S_IFDIR|0755, st_size=4096, ...}) = 0
close(3)                                  = 0
open("/usr/lib/locale/en_US.utf8/LC_MESSAGES/SYS_LC_MESSAGES",
O_RDONLY) = 3
fstat64(3, {st_mode=S_IFREG|0644, st_size=52, ...}) = 0
mmap2(NULL, 52, PROT_READ, MAP_PRIVATE, 3, 0) = 0xb75f6000
close(3)                                  = 0
...
```

Using the strace command to trace system calls

`strace` is a debugging tool that is used to trace system calls and signals. This information can used to troubleshoot problems with a command or program. The above example displays the typical output of the `strace` command. This output can be difficult to interpret; however, it is extremely helpful to developers when reporting bugs in a program.

> **Note** Some systems may use the `truss` command in place of `strace`.

Common usage examples:

`strace [PROGRAM]`	Trace the specified program
`strace -o [FILE] [PROGRAM]`	Save trace output to the specified file

ltrace

Purpose: Trace library calls.

Usage syntax: `ltrace [OPTIONS] [PROGRAM]`

```
$ ltrace ls
__libc_start_main(0x804e880, 1, 0xbfb04944, 0x8059e70, 0x8059e60
<unfinished ...>
setlocale(6, "")                                        = "en_US.UTF-8"
bindtextdomain("coreutils", "/usr/share/locale") = "/usr/share/locale"
textdomain("coreutils")                                 = "coreutils"
__cxa_atexit(0x8051b10, 0, 0, 0xb76dfff4, 0xbfb048a8) = 0
isatty(1)                                               = 0
getenv("QUOTING_STYLE")                                 = NULL
getenv("LS_BLOCK_SIZE")                                 = NULL
getenv("BLOCK_SIZE")                                    = NULL
getenv("BLOCKSIZE")                                     = NULL
getenv("POSIXLY_CORRECT")                               = NULL
getenv("BLOCK_SIZE")                                    = NULL
getenv("COLUMNS")                                       = NULL
ioctl(1, 21523, 0xbfb0487c)                             = -1
getenv("TABSIZE")                                       = NULL
getopt_long(1, 0xbfb04944, "abcdfghiklmnopqrstuvw:xABCDFGHI:"...,
0x805ca00, 0xbfb04890) = -1
__errno_location()                                      = 0xb757369c
malloc(36)                                              = 0x8065170
...
```

Using ltrace to debug a program

Similar to the previously discussed **strace** command, **ltrace** is a debugging tool for Linux systems that is used to trace library calls. The above example demonstrates the typical output of the **ltrace** command.

Common usage examples:

`ltrace [PROGRAM]`	Trace the specified program
`ltrace -o [FILE] [PROGRAM]`	Save trace output to the specified file

lsmod

Purpose: Display Linux kernel module information.

Usage syntax: `lsmod`

```
$ lsmod
Module                  Size   Used by
af_packet              23684   0
nfsd                  228720   13
auth_rpcgss            43424   1 nfsd
exportfs                6016   1 nfsd
nfs                   262156   0
lockd                  67720   3 nfsd,nfs
nfs_acl                 4608   2 nfsd,nfs
sunrpc                185500   11 nfsd,auth_rpcgss,nfs,lockd,nfs_acl
iptable_filter          3840   0
ip_tables              14820   1 iptable_filter
x_tables               16132   1 ip_tables
lp                     12324   0
loop                   19076   0
ipv6                  273188   18
parport_pc             36644   1
...
```

Output of the lsmod command

`lsmod` displays information about installed kernel modules. Kernel modules are an extension of the kernel itself. Each module generally serves a singular purpose, such as adding support for a specific technology or type of hardware. The above example displays the installed kernel modules on a Linux system.

`lsmod` is a Linux command. Similar commands exist on other platforms and are detailed in the following cross-reference table.

AIX	BSD	HP-UX	Linux	Solaris
gexkex	kldstat	kmadmin	lsmod	modinfo

Kernel module command cross-reference

Common usage examples:

`lsmod` | List installed kernel modules

insmod / rmmod

Purpose: Install/remove kernel modules.

Usage syntax: `insmod [MODULE]`

```
# insmod /lib/modules/2.6.24-27-server/kernel/drivers/block/floppy.ko
# lsmod | grep floppy
floppy                   59332  0
```
Loading a module into the kernel

The `insmod` command is used install to kernel modules on Linux systems. The above example demonstrates using `insmod` to install the `floppy.ko` module, which adds support to the system for floppy disk drives.

The `rmmod` command unloads modules from the kernel. The next example demonstrates removing the previously loaded `floppy.ko` module using the `rmmod` command.

Usage syntax: `rmmod [MODULE]`

```
# rmmod floppy
```
Removing a kernel module

`insmod` and `rmmod` are Linux commands. Similar commands exist on other platforms and are detailed in the following cross-reference table.

	BSD	HP-UX	Linux	Solaris
Install	kldload	kmadmin	insmod	modload
Remove	kldunload	kmadmin	rmmod	modunload

Kernel module command cross-reference

Common usage examples:

`insmod [MODULE]`	Load the specified module into the kernel
`rmmod [MODULE]`	Unload the specified module

modinfo

Purpose: Display information about Linux kernel modules.

Usage syntax: `modinfo [OPTIONS] [MODULE]`

```
$ modinfo nfs
filename:       /lib/modules/2.6.28-11-generic/kernel/fs/nfs/nfs.ko
license:        GPL
author:         Olaf Kirch <okir@monad.swb.de>
srcversion:     A400A43B7849FBE18225BCF
depends:        sunrpc,lockd,nfs_acl
vermagic:       2.6.28-11-generic SMP mod_unload modversions
parm:           enable_ino64:bool
```

Using the modinfo command to display information about the NFS module

`modinfo` displays information about Linux kernel modules. It includes helpful information such as the file location, license, version, and dependencies for the module. The above example demonstrates using **modinfo** to display information about the NFS kernel module.

Note	*Linux kernel modules typically are stored in the* `/var/lib/modules` *directory.*

Common usage examples:

`modinfo [MODULE]` | Display information about the specified module

sysctl

Purpose: Display and edit kernel parameters on Linux and BSD systems.

Usage syntax: `sysctl [OPTIONS]`

```
$ sysctl -a
kernel.sched_shares_ratelimit = 500000
kernel.sched_shares_thresh = 4
kernel.sched_child_runs_first = 1
kernel.sched_features = 24191
kernel.sched_migration_cost = 500000
kernel.sched_nr_migrate = 32
kernel.sched_rt_period_us = 1000000
kernel.sched_rt_runtime_us = 950000
kernel.sched_compat_yield = 0
kernel.panic = 0
kernel.core_uses_pid = 0
kernel.core_pattern = core
. . .
```

Displaying kernel parameters

The `sysctl` command displays and edits tunable kernel parameters. This allows you to fine tune various aspects of the operating system.

> **Warning**
> *You should not change these values unless you fully understand the impact of the parameter you are setting.*

Kernel parameters are typically stored in the `/etc/sysctl.conf` file. Settings changed on the command line via `sysctl` will be lost at reboot unless they are added to the `sysctl.conf` file.

> **Note**
> *HP-UX and Solaris use the `sysdef` command in place of `sysctl`. AIX systems use the `tunchange` command.*

Common usage examples:

`sysctl -a`	Display all kernel parameters
`sysctl -w [SETTING]=[VALUE]`	Set the specified kernel parameter

Section 13: Printing Commands

Overview

Commands in this section cover the basics of printer management on Unix, Linux, and BSD systems. The Unix printing subsystem is known as LPD (**L**ine **P**rinter **D**aemon). Linux uses a newer printing system called CUPS (**C**ommon **U**nix **P**rinting **S**ystem). Although these two printing services are very different at their core, they share mostly interchangeable commands.

Commands covered in this section:

Command	Purpose
lp	Print files.
lpstat	Display printer and print job status information.
lpq	Display print queue status.
cancel	Cancel and delete queued print jobs.
enable disable	Enable/disable printers.
lpadmin	Administer printers.

Glossary of terms used in this section:

CUPS	(**C**ommon **U**nix **P**rinting **S**ystem) A modern printing system for Unix, Linux, and BSD systems.
Print Job	A file that has been submitted for printing.
LPD	(**L**ine **P**rinter **D**aemon) Printing system used primarily on Unix and BSD systems.
Queue	A spooling system for print jobs waiting to be printed.

lp

Purpose: Print files.

Usage syntax: `lp [OPTIONS] [FILE]`

```
$ lp -d HP-4350 /etc/hosts
request id is HP-4350-4 (1 file(s))
```

Printing a file using the lp command

The `lp` command submits files for printing. In the above example, the `/etc/hosts` file is printed on the specified destination printer. The system will display a job summary after executing the command. Included in the job summary is the print job's ID number. On most systems, the ID number consists of the printer name with the job ID for the specified printer appended to it (4 in this case).

> **Note** *If no destination is specified, the file will print on the default system printer.*

Common usage examples:

`lp [FILE]`	Print a file to the default printer
`lp -d [PRINTER] [FILE]`	Print to the specified printer
`lp -n [NUM] -d [PRINTER] [FILE]`	Print the specified number of copies

lpstat

Purpose: Display printer and print job status information.

Usage syntax: `lpstat [OPTIONS]`

```
$ lpstat
HP-4350-5        nick        1024    Tue 02 Jun 2009 12:56:50 PM CDT
HP-4350-6        nick        1024    Tue 02 Jun 2009 12:56:51 PM CDT
HP-4350-7        nick        1024    Tue 02 Jun 2009 12:56:52 PM CDT
HP-4350-8        nick        1024    Tue 02 Jun 2009 12:56:52 PM CDT
```
Using the lpstat command to display queued print requests

The `lpstat` command displays information about printers and queued print jobs. In the above example, executing `lpstat` with no options displays the status of all queued print jobs.

The output of the `lpstat` command is defined in the following table.

Field 1	Field 2	Field 3	Field 4
PrinterName-JobID	Job owner	Job size	Submission time and date

The `-a` option shows the status of all printers on the local system as demonstrated in the next example.

```
$ lpstat -a
HP-4350 accepting requests since Tue 02 Jun 2009 12:51:08 PM CD
HP-5100 accepting requests since Tue 02 Jun 2009 12:51:08 PM CD
```
Displaying the status of all print queues on the local system

Common usage examples:

`lpstat`	Display the status of the print queue
`lpstat -a`	Display the current state of all printers
`lpstat -p`	Display the printing status of all printers
`lpstat -s`	Display a status summary
`lpstat -t`	Display all status information

lpq

Purpose: Display print queue status.

Usage syntax: `lpq [OPTIONS]`

```
$ lpq -a
Rank      Owner    Job    File(s)                         Total Size
1st       nick     2      hosts                           1024 bytes
2nd       nick     3      hosts                           1024 bytes
3rd       nick     4      hosts                           1024 bytes
4th       nick     5      hosts                           1024 bytes
5th       nick     6      hosts                           1024 bytes
6th       nick     7      hosts                           1024 bytes
7th       nick     8      hosts                           1024 bytes
8th       nick     9      hosts                           1024 bytes
9th       nick     10     hosts                           1024 bytes
```

Displaying the status of queued print jobs using the lpq command

The `lpq` command displays the status of queued print jobs. It is similar to the `lpstat` command except it provides more user-friendly output. Unlike the `lpstat` command, the `lpq` command only supports a limited number of command line options.

In the above example, executing `lpq -a` displays all queued print jobs. The next example demonstrates using the `-P` option to display the status of a specific printer.

```
$ lpq -P HP-4350
HP-4350 is not ready
Rank      Owner    Job    File(s)                         Total Size
1st       nick     2      hosts                           1024 bytes
2nd       nick     3      hosts                           1024 bytes
3rd       nick     4      hosts                           1024 bytes
4th       nick     5      hosts                           1024 bytes
```

Displaying the status of a specific printer using the lpq command

Common usage examples:

`lpq -a`	Display the status of all queued print jobs
`lpq -P [PRINTER]`	Display the status of the specified printer

cancel

Purpose: Cancel and delete queued print jobs.

Usage syntax: `cancel [OPTIONS] [JOBID]`

```
$ lpq -P HP-4350
HP-4350 is not ready
Rank      Owner    Job    File(s)                        Total Size
1st       nick     6      hosts                          1024 bytes
2nd       nick     7      hosts                          1024 bytes
3rd       nick     8      hosts                          1024 bytes
4th       nick     9      hosts                          1024 bytes
5th       nick     10     hosts                          1024 bytes
$ cancel 10
```

Using the cancel command to cancel an individual print job

The `cancel` command deletes queued print jobs. In the above example, `cancel` is used to remove an individual job by specifying the job's ID number. The next example demonstrates using the `-a` parameter to remove all queued print jobs from the specified printer.

```
$ lpq -P HP-4350
HP-4350 is not ready
Rank      Owner    Job    File(s)                        Total Size
1st       nick     6      hosts                          1024 bytes
2nd       nick     7      hosts                          1024 bytes
3rd       nick     8      hosts                          1024 bytes
4th       nick     9      hosts                          1024 bytes
$ cancel -a HP-4350
$ lpq -P HP-4350
HP-4350 is not ready
no entries
```

Using the cancel command to cancel all queued print jobs on a printer

> **Note** *Some UNIX systems may use the* `lprm` *command in place of* `cancel`.

Common usage examples:

`cancel [JOB]`	Cancel the specified print job
`cancel -a`	Cancel all print jobs on all printers
`cancel -a [PRINTER]`	Cancel all jobs on the specified printer

enable / disable

Purpose: Enable/disable printers.

Usage syntax: enable [OPTIONS] [PRINTER]

```
# enable HP-4350
# lpq
HP-4350 is ready
```
Enabling a printer using the enable command

The **enable** command enables printers which makes them available for printing. In the above example, the specified printer is enabled and made available for printing after executing the **enable** command.

The **disable** command takes printers offline and disables them from printing, as demonstrated in the next example.

Usage syntax: disable [OPTIONS] [PRINTER]

```
# disable HP-4350
# lpq
HP-4350 is not ready
```
Disabling a printer using the disable command

Most systems will continue to accept print requests when a printer is disabled. The jobs will remain in the queue until the printer is enabled.

> **Note** Systems with *CUPS (Common Unix Printing System)* will use the **cupsenable** *and* **cupsdisable** *commands in place of* **enable** *and* **disable**.

Common usage examples:

enable [PRINTER]	Enable the specified printer
disable [PRINTER]	Disable the specified printer
disable -c [PRINTER]	Disable a printer and cancel all queued jobs

lpadmin

Purpose: Administer printers.

Usage syntax: `lpadmin [OPTIONS] [PRINTER]`

```
$ lpadmin -p HP-5200 -E -v socket://10.10.1.32
$ lpstat -a
HP-5200 accepting requests since Fri 16 Apr 2010 12:41:01 PM CDT
```

Adding a printer using the lpadmin command

The `lpadmin` command manages printers on Unix, Linux, and BSD systems. In the above example, a network printer with the IP address of `10.10.1.32` is added to the system using the `lpadmin` command.

The next example demonstrates removing the printer created in the previous example using `lpadmin -x`.

```
$ lpadmin -x HP-5200
$ lpstat -a
```

Removing a printer using the lpadmin command

> **Note**
> *Command line options for the* `lpadmin` *utility vary across the different platforms. See* `man lpadmin` *for information specific to your system.*

Common usage examples:

`lpadmin -p [NAME] -v [DEVICE]`	Add a printer to the system
`lpadmin -x [PRINTER]`	Remove a printer from the system

Section 14:
Software Installation

Overview

Software installation is the one area that varies greatly across the different Unix, Linux, and BSD systems. Each distribution has its own unique set of software management utilities. This section provides an overview of these software management commands for each platform.

Commands covered in this section:

Command	Purpose
dpkg	Install /remove Debian Linux software packages.
aptitude	Automated package manager for Debian Linux-based systems.
rpm	Install /remove Red Hat Linux packages.
yum	Automated package manager for Red Hat Linux-based systems.
emerge	Install/remove Gentoo Linux packages.
pkg_add pkg_delete	Install/remove BSD packages.
pkg_info	Display information about BSD packages.
installp	Install software packages on AIX systems.
lslpp	List installed software on AIX systems.
pkgadd pkgrm	Install/remove Solaris packages.
pkginfo	List installed packages on Sun Solaris systems.
make	Compile and install software from source code.

Glossary of terms used in this section:

APT	(**A**dvanced **P**ackaging **T**ool) A package manager used on Debian Linux-based systems.
Compile	The process of converting source code into a binary/executable file.
Dependency	A program or library required in order for another program to function properly.
Makefile	A file used during the compilation of software.
Package	A self contained file used for software installation.
Portage	Package manager used on Gentoo Linux-based systems.
Repository	A source of packages used by a package management program.
RPM	(**R**ed **H**at **P**ackage **M**anager) A software package format created by Red Hat, Inc.

dpkg

Purpose: Install/remove Debian Linux software packages.

Usage syntax: dpkg [OPTIONS] [FILE]

```
# dpkg -i apache2_amd64.deb
Preparing to install apache2 (using apache2_amd64.deb).
Unpacking apache2.
Setting up apache2.
Processing triggers for man-db ...
Processing triggers for ufw ...
...
```

Installing the Apache web server package using dpkg

dpkg is the traditional package manager for Debian Linux-based systems. It can be found on Debian and Ubuntu as well as a host of other Linux distributions built on the Debian core.

Using dpkg, you can install or remove programs created specifically for Debian-based systems. These packages typically have a .deb file extension. The above example demonstrates using the dpkg command to install a Debian package.

Note	*Most Debian-based systems now utilize a program called* aptitude *to perform software installation tasks. Directly installing packages using dpkg is rarely done given that aptitude will automatically download and install the requested package(s) and all required dependencies. See page 246 for more information.*

Common usage examples:

dpkg -i [PACKAGE]	Install the specified package
dpkg -r [PACKAGE]	Remove the specified package
dpkg -p [PACKAGE]	Remove the specified package and related config files
dpkg -l	List all installed packages

aptitude

Purpose: Automated package manager for Debian Linux-based systems.

Usage syntax: `aptitude [OPTIONS] [ACTION] [PACKAGE]`

```
# aptitude install apache2
Reading package lists... Done
Building dependency tree
Reading state information... Done
The following extra packages will be installed:
   apache2-mpm-worker apache2-utils apache2.2-common libapr1 libaprutil1
libpq5
Suggested packages:
   apache2-doc apache2-suexec apache2-suexec-custom
The following NEW packages will be installed:
   apache2 apache2-mpm-worker apache2-utils apache2.2-common libapr1
   libaprutil1 libpq5
0 upgraded, 7 newly installed, 0 to remove and 13 not upgraded.
After this operation, 6382kB of additional disk space will be used.
Do you want to continue [Y/n]? Y
...
```

Installing the Apache web server with aptitude

aptitude is a front-end for the Debian **dpkg** package manager. It simplifies software installation by automatically downloading and installing packages and any required dependencies. In this example, the **aptitude** program will automatically download and install the packages required to run the Apache web server application.

> **Note** *Software repositories listed in `/etc/apt/sources.list` are used to query the package database for available programs and their download locations.*

Common usage examples:

`aptitude update`	Update the package database
`aptitude upgrade`	Install the newest versions of all packages
`aptitude dist-upgrade`	Upgrade the entire distribution
`aptitude install [PACKAGE]`	Install the specified package
`aptitude remove [PACKAGE]`	Remove the specified package
`aptitude search [NAME]`	Search repositories for a package by name
`aptitude show [PACKAGE]`	Display information about a package
`aptitude clean`	Clean the package cache
`aptitude --purge-unused`	Remove unused packages

rpm

Purpose: Install/remove Red Hat Linux packages.

Usage syntax: `rpm [OPTIONS] [FILE]`

```
# rpm -iv nmap-4.85BETA9-1.i386.rpm
Preparing packages for installation...
nmap-4.85BETA9-1
...
```

Installing the nmap program using the rpm command

rpm is the traditional package manager for Red Hat Linux-based systems. It can be found on Red Hat Enterprise Linux and Fedora as well as a host of other Linux distributions built on the Red Hat/Fedora core.

Using **rpm** you can install or remove programs created specifically for Red Hat and Fedora-based systems. These packages typically have a `.rpm` file extension. The above example demonstrates using the **rpm** command to install an RPM package.

> **Note**
>
> *Most Red Hat-based systems now utilize a program called **yum** to perform software installation tasks. Directly installing packages using **rpm** is rarely done given that **yum** will automatically download and install the requested package(s) and all required dependencies. See page 248 for more information.*

Common usage examples:

`rpm -i [PACKAGE]`	Install the specified package
`rpm -U [PACKAGE]`	Upgrade the specified package
`rpm -e [PACKAGE]`	Remove the specified package
`rpm -qa`	List all installed packages

yum

Purpose: Automated package manager for Red Hat Linux-based systems.

Usage syntax: yum [OPTIONS] [PACKAGE]

```
# yum install nmap
Loaded plugins: refresh-packagekit
Setting up Install Process
Resolving Dependencies
--> Running transaction check
---> Package nmap.i586 2:4.76-4.fc11 set to be updated
--> Finished Dependency Resolution
...
```

Installing a software package with the yum package manager

yum is a front-end for the Red Hat Linux **rpm** package manager. It simplifies software installation by automatically downloading and installing packages and any required dependencies. In this example, the **yum** command will automatically download and install the packages required to run the **nmap** utility.

> **Note** Software repositories listed in /etc/yum.conf are used to query the package database for available packages and their download locations.

Common usage examples:

yum install [PACKAGE]	Install the specified package
yum remove [PACKAGE]	Remove the specified package
yum update	Install the newest versions of all packages
yum upgrade	Upgrade the distribution to the latest version
yum list	List available and installed packages
yum search [NAME]	Search for the specified package by name

emerge

Purpose: Install/remove Gentoo Linux packages.

Usage syntax: emerge [OPTIONS] [PACKAGE]

```
# emerge uptime
Calculating dependencies... done!
>>> Verifying ebuild Manifests...
>>> Emerging (1 of 1) app-vim/uptime-1.3 to /
>>> Downloading 'http://distfiles.gentoo.org/distfiles/uptime-
1.3.tar.bz2'
...
```

Installing the uptime utility on Gentoo Linux using the emerge program

emerge is a front-end for Gentoo's Portage software manager. It provides automatic software compilation, installation, and dependency fulfillment similar to the previously discussed **aptitude** and **yum** commands.

Portage is a unique package manager in the fact that it compiles software from source code. This is different than most other Linux systems which utilize precompiled binaries when installing software. Compiling software from source code creates a platform-optimized installation that has been shown to provide better performance when compared to precompiled packages. Portage's disadvantage, however, is that it takes much longer to install software for source.

| Tip | *To learn more about the Portage software manager, see the official Gentoo documentation online at www.gentoo.org/doc/.* |

Common usage examples:

emerge [PACKAGE]	Install the specified package
emerge -u world	Install the newest versions of all packages
emerge -C [PACKAGE]	Remove the specified package
emerge -s [PACKAGE]	Search for the specified package
emerge --sync	Update the portage database

pkg_add / pkg_delete

Purpose: Install/remove BSD packages.

Usage syntax: `pkg_add [OPTIONS] [PACKAGE]`

```
# pkg_add -r perl
Fetching ftp://ftp.freebsd.org/pub/FreeBSD/ports/i386/packages-7.2-
release/Latest/perl.tbz...
Creating various symlinks in /usr/bin...
    Symlinking /usr/local/bin/perl5.8.9 to /usr/bin/perl
...
```

Installing a package using the pkg_add command

The `pkg_add` command installs software packages on BSD systems. In the above example, `pkg_add` is used to install a package called Perl. The `-r` option instructs `pkg_add` to retrieve the specified package automatically from the BSD software repository.

> **Tip**
>
> The `pkg_add` command uses the default FTP server located at ftp.freebsd.org. For faster download you can specify an FTP mirror using the `PACKAGEROOT` environment variable. For example, typing `export PACKAGEROOT=ftp.ca.freebsd.org` would instruct the `pkg_add` command to use the specified mirror located in Canada. A complete list of FTP mirror sites can be found online at http://mirrorlist.freebsd.org/FBSDsites.php.

The `pkg_delete` command uninstalls software packages on BSD systems. In the next example, the previously installed Perl package is removed using the `pkg_delete` command.

Usage syntax: `pkg_delete [PACKAGE]`

```
# pkg_delete perl-5.8.9_2
Removing stale symlinks from /usr/bin...
    Removing /usr/bin/perl
    Removing /usr/bin/perl5... Done.
...
```

Removing a package using the pkg_delete command

Common usage examples:

`pkg_add -r [PACKAGE]` | Download and install the specified package
`pkg_delete [PACKAGE]` | Uninstall the specified package

pkg_info

Purpose: Display information about BSD packages.

Usage syntax: pkg_info [OPTIONS]

```
# pkg_info
bash-4.0.33            The GNU Project's Bourne Again SHell
en-freebsd-doc-20090913 Documentation from the FreeBSD Documentation
Project
gettext-0.17_1         GNU gettext package
libiconv-1.13.1        A character set conversion library
lua-5.1.4              Small, compilable scripting language providing easy
access
nano-2.0.9_1           Nano's ANOther editor, an enhanced free Pico clone
nmap-5.00              Port scanning utility for large networks
pcre-7.9               Perl Compatible Regular Expressions library
perl-5.8.9_3           Practical Extraction and Report Language
pkg-config-0.23_1      A utility to retrieve information about installed
libraries
```

Displaying information about installed packages using the pkg_info command

The `pkg_info` command displays information about installed packages on BSD systems. In the above example, executing `pkg_info` with no options generates a simple list of installed programs.

Executing the `pkg_info` command with the `-a` option displays detailed information about the installed packages as displayed in the next example.

```
# pkg_info nmap-5.00 | less
Information for nmap-5.00:

Comment:
Port scanning utility for large networks

Description:
Nmap is a utility for network exploration and security auditing.
...
```

Using the pkg_info command to display information about a specific package

Common usage examples:

pkg_info	Display a simple list of installed packages
pkg_info -a	Display a detailed list of installed packages
pkg_info [PACKAGE]	Display information about the specified package

installp

Purpose: Install software packages on AIX systems.

Usage syntax: `installp [OPTIONS] [PACKAGE]`

```
# installp -Y -d /mnt/cdrom httpd.base
...
Installation Summary
--------------------
Name                Level          Part        Event       Result
-----------------------------------------------------------------
httpd.base          2.2.6.0        USR         APPLY       SUCCESS
```
Installing the Apache http server on AIX

The `installp` command installs software packages on AIX systems. The above example demonstrates installing the Apache web server package located on the install media mounted in `/mnt/cdrom`.

> **Note**
>
> The `-Y` option accepts any required license agreements during installation.

To remote a package, use the `-u` option as demonstrated in the next example.

```
# installp -u httpd.base
...
Installation Summary
--------------------
Name                Level          Part        Event       Result
-----------------------------------------------------------------
httpd.base          2.2.6.0        USR         DEINSTALL   SUCCESS
```
Removing a package on AIX

Common usage examples:

`installp -ld [MEDIA]`	List packages on the specified media
`installp -Yd [PATH] [PACKAGE]`	Install the specified package
`installp -u [PACKAGE]`	Uninstall the specified package

lslpp

Purpose: List installed software on AIX systems.

Usage syntax: `lslpp [OPTIONS] [PACKAGE]`

```
# lslpp -L httpd.base
  Fileset                      Level   State  Type  Description (Uninstaller)
  ----------------------------------------------------------------------------
  httpd.base                   2.2.6.0   C      F   Apache Http Server


State codes:
  A -- Applied.
  B -- Broken.
  C -- Committed.
  E -- EFIX Locked.
  O -- Obsolete.  (partially migrated to newer version)
  ? -- Inconsistent State...Run lppchk -v.

Type codes:
  F -- Installp Fileset
  P -- Product
  C -- Component
  T -- Feature
  R -- RPM Package
  E -- Interim Fix
```

Listing an installed package on AIX

The `lslpp` command lists installed software on AIX systems. The example above demonstrates using `lslpp` to list the installation status of the `httpd.base` package.

> **Note** *Omitting a package name will list all installed software on the system.*

Common usage examples:

`lslpp -L`	List all installed packages
`lslpp -L [PACKAGE]`	List the specified install package

pkgadd / pkgrm

Purpose: Install/remove Solaris packages.

Usage syntax: `pkgadd [OPTIONS] [PATH]`

```
# pkgadd -d /cdrom/sol_10_1009_x86/Solaris_10/Product/

The following packages are available:
...
 91  SUNWapch2d              Apache Web Server V2 Documentation
                             (i386) 11.10.0,REV=2005.01.08.01.09
 92  SUNWapch2r              Apache Web Server V2 (root)
                             (i386) 11.10.0,REV=2005.01.08.01.09
 93  SUNWapch2u              Apache Web Server V2 (usr)
                             (i386) 11.10.0,REV=2005.01.08.01.09
 94  SUNWapchS               Source for the Apache httpd server
                             (i386) 11.10.0,REV=2005.01.08.01.09
...
Select package(s) you wish to process (or 'all' to process
all packages). (default: all) [?,??,q]: 92
...
Installation of <SUNWapch2r> was successful.
```

Installing a software package on Solaris

The **pkgadd** command installs software packages on Solaris systems. The example above demonstrates using **pkgadd** to install packages from the Solaris installation media.

The **pkgrm** command removes packages on Solaris systems. The next example demonstrates removing a package using **pkgrm**.

Usage syntax: `pkgrm [OPTIONS] [PACKAGE]`

```
# pkgrm SUNWapch2r

The following package is currently installed:
   SUNWapch2r  Apache Web Server V2 (root)
               (i386) 11.10.0,REV=2005.01.08.01.09

Do you want to remove this package? [y,n,?,q]
...
Removal of <SUNWapch2r> was successful.
```

Removing a package on Solaris

Common usage examples:

`pkgadd -d [PATH]`	Install packages from the specified location
`pkgrm [PACKAGE]`	Remove the specified package

254

pkginfo

Purpose: List installed packages on Sun Solaris systems.

Usage syntax: `pkginfo [OPTIONS] [PACKAGE]`

```
# pkginfo | more
system       BRCMbnx        Broadcom NetXtreme II Gigabit Ethernet
system       CADP160        Adaptec Ultra160 SCSI Host Adapter Driver
system       HPFC           Agilent Fibre Channel HBA Driver
system       NCRos86r       NCR Platform Support, OS Functionality
system       NVDAgraphics   NVIDIA Graphics System Software
system       NVDAgraphicsr  NVIDIA Graphics System Device Driver
system       SK98sol        SysKonnect SK-NET Gigabit Ethernet Adapter
system       SKfp           SysKonnect PCI-FDDI Host Adapter
system       SUNW1251f      Russian 1251 fonts
system       SUNW1394       Sun IEEE1394 Framework
system       SUNW1394h      Sun IEEE1394 Framework Header Files
system       SUNWGlib       GLIB - Library of useful routines for C
system       SUNWGtkr       GTK - The GIMP Toolkit (Root)
system       SUNWGtku       GTK - The GIMP Toolkit (Usr)
GNOME2       SUNWPython     The Python interpreter, libraries and
...
```

Listing installed packages on Solaris systems

The `pkginfo` command lists installed packages on Solaris systems. Executing `pkginfo` with no options lists all installed packages as demonstrated in the above example. Specifying a package name will list the package as shown in the next example.

```
# pkginfo SUNWapch2r
system       SUNWapch2r Apache Web Server V2 (root)
```

Displaying a specific package using pkginfo

Common usage examples:

`pkginfo`	List all installed software packages
`pkginfo [PACKAGE]`	List the specified software package

make

Purpose: Compile and install software from source code.

Usage syntax: `make [OPTIONS] [FILE]`

```
# ls -l Makefile
-r--r--r-- 1 nick nick 1636 2007-08-10 13:48 Makefile
# make && make install
*** stopping make sense ***
make[1]: Entering directory '/home/nick/Desktop/chkrootkit-0.48'
gcc -DHAVE_LASTLOG_H -o chklastlog chklastlog.c
chklastlog.c: In function 'main':
chklastlog.c:167: warning: format '%ld' expects type 'long int', but
option 3 has type 'int'
chklastlog.c:167: warning: format '%ld' expects type 'long int', but
option 4 has type 'uid_t'
gcc -DHAVE_LASTLOG_H -o chkwtmp chkwtmp.c
...
```

Manually compiling software from source code using make

The **make** command compiles and installs programs from source code. Source code compatible with the **make** command is distributed with what is known as a Makefile. The Makefile is a script used to build and install the source code using the **make** command.

In the above example, the **make** and **make install** commands are combined to build the source code of a program and install it.

Note	*Most users will never have to compile software from source since major distributions provide prebuilt packages for nearly every program available. Additionally, Linux tools such as* **yum***,* **apt***, and* **emerge** *greatly simplify software installation and dependency fulfillment.*

Common usage examples:

`make`	Compile source code
`make install`	Install compiled source code

Section 15:
System Administration Utilities

Overview

This section coverers two very helpful system administration utilities for commercial Unix systems:

- **SMIT**: **S**ystem **M**anagement **I**nterface **T**ool for AIX
- **SAM**: **S**ystem **A**dministration **M**anager for HP-UX

SMIT and SAM are menu-driven applications that can be used to simplify complex administration tasks such as managing hardware, software, users/groups, etc. While every task that can be performed in SMIT or SAM can be executed on the command line, running the same task within these utilities is generally much easier and faster. They also provide an added layer of protection from mistakes by ensuring that the requested task is executed with the correct parameters.

Commands covered in this section:

Command	Purpose
sam	HP-UX System Administration Manager
smit	AIX System Management Interface Tool

sam

Purpose: Menu-driven system administration utility for HP-UX systems.

Usage syntax: sam

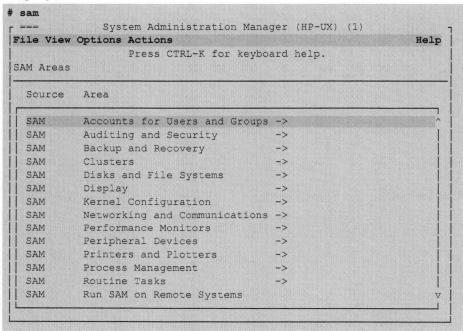

Screenshot of the HP-UX System Administration Manager

sam is a menu-driven administration utility for HP-UX systems. It can be used to manage all aspects of an HP-UX system.

The above example displays a screen shot of the main menu in **sam**. Within **sam**, the arrow keys are used to navigate the menus and the **Enter** key is used to select items. Pressing the **Tab** key activates the menu bar at the top of the screen allowing access to additional features.

Common usage examples:

sam	Start the HP-UX system administration manager

smit

Purpose: Menu-driven system administration utility for IBM AIX systems.

Usage syntax: `smit`

```
# smit
                        System Management
Move cursor to desired item and press Enter.
[TOP]
   Software Installation and Maintenance
   Software License Management
   Devices
   System Storage Management (Physical & Logical Storage)
   Security & Users
   Communications Applications and Services
   Workload Partition Administration
   Print Spooling
   Advanced Accounting
   Problem Determination
   Performance & Resource Scheduling
   System Environments
   Processes & Subsystems
   Applications
   Installation Assistant
[MORE...3]
F1=Help                 F2=Refresh              F3=Cancel              F8=Image
F9=Shell                F10=Exit                Enter=Do
```

Screenshot of the IBM AIX System Management Interface Tool

`smit` is a menu-driven administration utility for IBM AIX systems. It can be used to manage all aspects of an AIX system.

The above example displays a screen shot of the main menu in `smit`. Within `smit`, the arrow keys are used to navigate the menus and the **Enter** key is used to select items. Function keys (i.e., **F1**, **F2**, etc.) provide additional options within `smit` and are defined at the bottom of each screen.

Common usage examples:

`smit` | Start the AIX system management interface tool

Appendix A:
Bash Shortcut Keys

Download and print this list at www.dontfearthecommandline.com

Key(s)	Function
CTRL + C	Terminate current program
CTRL + Z	Suspend current program
CTRL + D	Exit the current shell
Tab	Command/file auto-completion
Home	Go to the beginning of the command line
End	Go to the end of the command line
CTRL + L	Clear the screen
Backspace	Deletes text behind the cursor
ATL + Backspace	Delete entire word behind the cursor
Delete	Delete text in front of the cursor
CTRL + R	Search command history
Up Arrow	Cycle backward through command history
Down Arrow	Cycle forward through command history
Left Arrow	Move the cursor left one character
Right Arrow	Move the cursor right one character
ALT + B	Move the cursor back one word
ALT + F	Move the cursor forward one word
CTRL + U	Cut all text before the cursor
CTRL + K	Cut all text after the cursor
ALT + D	Cut the currently selected word
CTRL + Y	Paste previously cut text
CTRL + _ (Underscore)	Undo changes typed on the command line
CTRL + T	Transpose the previous two characters on the command line
ALT + T	Transpose the previous two words on the command line
ATL + L	Convert word to lowercase
ATL + U	Convert word to uppercase

Appendix B:
Command Line Cheat Sheet

Download and print this list at www.dontfearthecommandline.com

Help Commands

man	Online manual
whatis	Display manual descriptions

File and Directory Commands

ls	Lists directory contents
pwd	Prints the current directory
cd	Change directories
mv	Move files
cp	Copy files
rm	Delete files
mkdir	Create directories
rmdir	Remove directories
find	Search for files (slow)
locate	Search for files (faster)
whereis	Display binary file location
file	Display file type
tree	Display directory tree
stat	Display file statistics
fuser	Identify open files
touch	Update file timestamps
lsof	List open files
cksum	Calculate checksum
md5sum	Calculate md5sum
ln	Create a link
alias	Display/edit command aliases
gzip	Compress files
gunzip	Uncompress files
shred	Securely delete files
head	Display the head of a file
tail	Display the tail of a file
tee	Display and redirect output
sort	Sort input files/streams
grep	Display matching results
split	Split a file into multiple parts
more	Display files one page at a time
less	Display files one page at a time
wc	Count words/lines/letters
cat	Concatenate files
tac	Reverse concatenate files
zcat	Display compressed files

diff	Show differences between files
strings	Display printable characters
sed	Text editing utility
awk	Text processing utility
dos2unix	Convert DOS files to Unix
unix2dos	Convert Unix files to DOS

Editors

nano	Simple text editor
vi/vim	Advanced text editor
emacs	Ultimate text editor

Other Utilities

clear	Clear terminal screen
date	Display the date
cal	Display a calendar
watch	Monitor a command
env	Display environment variables
history	Display command history
logout	Log out of the shell
exit	Exit the shell

Users and Groups

su	Switch users
sudo	Run a program as another user
id	Display user identity
ulimit	Display user limits
groups	Display a user's groups
who	Display who is logged in
w	Display what users are doing
whoami	Display current user id
last	Display last user logins
lastb	Display failed user logins
lastlog	Display all users' last logins
wall	Send a message to all users
finger	Display information about a user
chown	Change file/directory ownership
chgrp	Change file/directory group
chmod	Change file permissions
umask	Display or set umask settings
passwd	Set/change password

useradd	Create user accounts
userdel	Delete user accounts
usermod	Modify user accounts
adduser	Create user accounts (Linux)
deluser	Delete user accounts (Linux)
groupadd	Create group accounts
groupdel	Delete group accounts
groupmod	Modify group accounts

Process Control

ps	Display running processes
pgrep	Search for running processes
pstree	Display process in tree view
kill	Terminate a process by PID
killall	Terminal a process by name
nice	Run a program with a modified priority
renice	Adjust a program's priority
nohup	Run a program immune to hang-ups
&	Run a program in the background
bg	Move a job to the background
jobs	Display running jobs
fg	Move a job to the foreground

Scheduling

batch	Run processes when the CPU is free
at	Run processes at a specific time
atq	Display the at queue
atrm	Remove jobs from the at queue
crontab	Display/edit cron jobs

Startup and Shutdown

shutdown	Shutdown the computer
poweroff	Poweroff the computer
reboot	Reboot the system
halt	Halt the computer
runlevel	Display the current runlevel
telinit	Change runlevel
service	Stop and stop services
sysv-rc-conf	Runlevel configuration editor
chkconfig	Red Hat runlevel editor
rc-update	Change Gentoo services
rc-status	Display Gentoo services
stopsrc	Stop AIX services
startsrc	Start AIX services
lssrc	List AIX services
svcs	List Solaris services
svcadm	Manage Solaris services

Networking Commands

hostname	Display the system hostname
ifconfig	Manage network interfaces
ifup	Start network interfaces
ifdown	Stop network interfaces
iwconfig	Manage wireless interfaces
ethtool	Display network card info
arp	Display the ARP cache
ping	Send ICMP echo requests
traceroute	Trace network paths
tracepath	Trace network paths
nslookup	Query DNS servers
dig	Query DNS servers
host	Query DNS servers
whois	Query the whois database
dhclient	Linux DHCP client
ifstat	Display network statistics
netstat	Display network status
route	Manage network routes
tcpdump	Capture network packets
nmap	Scan remote computers
showmount	Show mounted file systems
ssh	SSH client
telnet	Telnet client
ftp	FTP client
mail	Email client
wget	File download utility
minicom	Serial communication utility

Hardware Commands

lspci	List PCI devices
pciconf	List PCI devices
lsusb	List USB devices
lshw	List hardware devices
dmidecode	Display all system hardware
hdparm	Configure hard drives
eject	Eject removable media
ioscan	List HP-UX devices
lsdev	List AIX devices

File System Commands

fdisk	Partition editor
parted	Partition editor
mkfs	Create file systems
fsck	Check file systems
mkswap	Create swap space
swapon	Activate swap space
swapoff	Deactivate swap space
sync	Flush disk cache
mount	Mount file systems
swapinfo	Display swap information

tune2fs	Tune linux file systems
umount	Unmount file systems
badblocks	Check a disk for bad blocks

Printing Commands

lp	Print files
lpstat	Display printer status
lpq	Display print queue
lpadmin	Configure printers
cancel	Cancel print jobs
enable	Enable a printer (LPD)
disable	Disable a printer (LDP)
cupsenable	Enable a printer (CUPS)
cupsdisable	Disable a printer (CUPS)

Backup Commands

tar	Archive utility
dd	File copy utility
dump	Incremental backup utility
restore	Restore dump backups
mt	Tape device utility
cpio	Archive utility
mksysb	AIX backup utility

Monitoring Commands

top	Performance monitor
topas	AIX performance monitor
htop	Linux performance monitor
mpstat	Performance monitor
vmstat	Virtual memory monitor
iostat	I/O performance monitor
iotop	Linux I/O monitor
nfsstat	NFS performance monitor
free	Display memory usage
df	Display disk usage
du	Display disk usage
uname	Display system information
uptime	Display system uptime
dmesg	Display kernel messages
strace	System trace debugger
ltrace	Library trace debugger
sysctl	Configure kernel parameters
dstat	Linux system monitor
errpt	Display the AIX error log
insmod	Install kernel modules
rmmod	Remove kernel modules
lsmod	List kernel modules
modinfo	Display module information

Software Commands

dpkg	Debian package manager
aptitude	Debian package utility
rpm	Red Hat package manager
yum	Red Hat package utility
emerge	Gentoo package utility
pkg_add	BSD installation utility
pkg_delete	BSD uninstallation utility
pkg_info	Display BSD packages
swinstall	HP-UX installation utility
swlist	Display HP-UX packages
swremove	HP-UX uninstallation utility
installp	AIX installation utility
lslpp	Display AIX packages
pkgadd	Solaris installation utility
pkgrm	Solaris uninstallation utility
pkginfo	Display Solaris packages
make	Compile software from source

Administration Utilities

sam	HP-UX administration utility
smit	AIX administration utility

Appendix C: Command Cross Reference

Commands such as `ls`, `rm`, and `mv` are universal across all Unix, Linux, and BSD systems. Other commands used for installing/removing software, managing, hardware, and other administrative tasks differ from system to system. The table below provides a cross-reference for these platform specific commands.

	AIX	BSD	HP-UX	Linux	Solaris
List Hardware	lsdev	pciconf	ioscan	lspci	prtconf
List modules	gexkex	kldstat	kmadmin	lsmod	modinfo
Add modules		kldload	kmadmin	insmod	modload
Remove Modules		kldunload	kmadmin	rmmod	modunload
List Swap Space	lsps	swapinfo	swapinfo	free	swap
Add Swap Space	mkps	swapctl	lvcreate	mkswap	swap
Remove Swap Space	rmps	swapctl	lvremove	fdisk parted	swap
Activate Swap Space	swapon	swapon	swapon	swapon	swap
Deactivate Swap Space	swapoff	swapoff	swapoff	swapoff	swap
Start Services	startsrc		sam	service	svcadm
Stop Services	stopsrc		sam	service	svcadm
List Services	lssrc		sam	sysv-rc-conf chkconfig	svcs
List Installed Software	lslpp	pkg_info	swlist	dpkg -i rpm -qa	pkginfo
Install software	installp	pkg_add	swinstall	aptitude yum	pkgadd
Remove software	installp -u	pkg_delete	swremove	aptitude yum	pkgrm
Error Reporting	errpt	dmesg	dmesg	dmesg	dmesg
Performance Monitor	topas	top	top	top	top
Admin Utility	smit		sam		
Partition Editor	smit	fdisk	sam	fdisk parted	format

Now available at NmapCookBook.com

Nmap® Cookbook: *The Fat-Free Guide to Network Scanning*

The Nmap Cookbook provides simplified coverage of network scanning features available in the Nmap suite of utilities. Every Nmap feature is covered with visual examples to help you quickly understand and identify proper usage for practical results.

www.NmapCookBook.com

17883880R00144

Made in the USA
Lexington, KY
02 October 2012